Independent Schools
Examinations Board

HISTORY PRACTICE EXERCISES 13+ ANSWER BOOK

Gavin Hannah

Independent Schools
Examinations Board

www.galorepark.co.uk

GALORE PARK

Published by ISEB Publications, an imprint of Galore Park Publishing Ltd
19/21 Sayers Lane, Tenterden, Kent TN30 6BW
www.galorepark.co.uk

Design and typography by Typetechnique
Printed by Charlesworth Press, Wakefield

ISBN: 978 1907047 00 8

First published 2009, reprinted 2011, 2012

Details of other ISEB publications, examination papers and Galore Park
publications are available at www.galorepark.co.uk

Contents

Introduction v

Answers to Evidence Questions 1

A. Medieval Realms: Britain 1066–1485 1

    The First Crusade 1

    Matilda and Stephen 1

    Richard the Lionheart 2

    King John 3

    Edward I, Wales and Scotland 3

    Edward II and Scotland 4

    The Black Death 1348–1350 5

    Henry V 5

    Women in Medieval Society 6

B. The Making of the United Kingdom: 1485–1750 7

    Henry VII 7

    Henry VIII 7

    Henry VIII and his Great Matter 8

    Lady Jane Grey and Mary I 9

    Mary I and the Protestants 9

    Elizabeth I 10

    The Causes of the Civil War 1629–1641 11

    The Battle of Marston Moor 11

    The Plague of London 1665 12

    James II and the Glorious Revolution 12

    The Jacobite Rebellion of 1745 13

C. Britain: 1750–circa 1900 14

    The French Revolution 14

    The Battle of Waterloo 14

The Great Reform Bill of 1832 15

Chartism 16

The Crimean War 16

The Indian Mutiny 17

The Cotton Industry 18

Trade Unions 18

Slavery and the Triangular Trade 19

The British Empire 20

Answers to Essay Questions 21

A. Medieval Realms: Britain 1066–1485 21

War and Rebellion 21

Government and Parliament 28

Religion 32

Social History 36

General Topics 38

B. The Making of the United Kingdom: 1485–1750 42

War and Rebellion 42

Government and Parliament 49

Religion 58

Social History 66

General Topics 71

C. Britain 1750–circa 1900 76

War and Rebellion 76

Government and Parliament 84

Religion and Social Reform 88

Social and Economic History 90

General Topics 97

Appendix – ISEB Common Entrance 13+ Mark Scheme 105

Introduction

History Practice Exercises: 13+ Answer Book offers worked examples of the answers to the evidence and essay questions across the whole syllabus from 1066 to 1900, as presented in *History Practice Exercises 13+* by Gavin Hannah and Paul Spencer, ISBN: 9780903627771 (Galore Park, 2009).

Evidence Questions

The answers to the evidence questions have been written out in full. Each one was produced in 20 minutes, which is the normal time suggested by the setters for tackling such exercises. They might be considered too long by some of you. In my defence, I would say that they have all been written out by hand, in my large, scrawly scribble. They show what can be done and are something which pupils might aspire to.

None of the answers is perfect. Indeed, there are plenty of alternative ways of earning the marks. This is, of course, both the beauty (and one of the difficulties) of history. For example, in question 4, many may disagree with my choice of the most, or the least, useful source.

Questions 1 and 2 are straightforward comprehension exercises. The second response should be a little longer, with a word or two to justify the answer. Pupils should use the mark scheme to help them gauge how much to write.

Question 3: pupils should be clear in their mind what Source C is saying. Then they will be able to compare it to A and B. They should not forget the **differences** as well as the **similarities**.

Question 4: pupils should discuss **each** source carefully and must not miss any out. They need to say something about the source in relation to the question, and discuss its **provenance**. This will help rate its accuracy, its reliability and, from there, its usefulness (utility).

The answers offered here are meant to show what **reasoned discussion and analysis** look like. Pupils should look at the style of the answers, particularly to questions 3 and 4.

Essay Questions

The essays have been presented in bullet-point form. This is partly to save space. Also, I do not want to impose my writing style on what you might expect from a pupil. **Please remember that in the real examination, pupils must write out essays in full**.

An essay written out fully should normally be produced in **35 minutes**, as suggested by the setters.

Understanding and Using the Mark Scheme

The Independent Schools Examinations Board provides a **mark scheme** as guidance for examiners assessing History Common Entrance scripts. A copy of this scheme may be found in the Appendix on page 105. The Board makes the point that it is a 'suggested' rather than a 'prescriptive' scheme. Nonetheless, it is useful. It should be studied by teachers, pupils, tutors, parents and anyone else helping with examination preparation. The mark scheme shows exactly **what is expected** for answers to merit the highest marks. It indicates also what should **not** be done. Following its advice greatly increases the chances of attaining that top-grade pass!

Evidence Questions

Questions 1 and 2 of the evidence question are assessed at either level 1 or level 2. Questions 3 and 4 are rated at level 1, level 2 or level 3. All the suggested answers in this book have been written as examples of the highest levels. That is to say, at level 2 for questions 1 and 2 and at level 3 for questions 3 and 4.

However, examples of the lower levels for one evidence question are offered here as guidance towards the top band. The evidence question concerning *The Black Death 1348–1350* may be found on pages 14–15 of the pupils' book. A suggested 'top level' answer appears in this book on page 5. This should be compared with what follows.

1. Look at **Source A**. Give one reason why the families of plague victims had to bury their own dead. (2)

Level 1 answer	Comments
Because lots of people died.	Answer is both incomplete and imprecise. One mark.

2. Look at **Source B**. Describe two kinds of plague symptoms mentioned by the writer. (3)

Level 1 answer	Comments
Some victims had boils.	Incomplete answer offering only one symptom. One mark.

3. Look carefully at **Source C**. With which source, **A** or **B**, does it most agree concerning the plague? (7)

Level 1 answer	Comments
Source C shows people fleeing from their village and a man with the plague.	Answer makes only a basic comment on this source. There is no attempt at comparison which is the whole point of question 3. One mark.

Level 2 answer	Comments
Source **C** shows a man with spots all over his body. This agrees with what is mentioned in **B** about people having spots full of puss all over their bodies when they had the plague.	This is a more developed answer. There is evidence of comparison between the two sources and some attempt at substantiated argument. Answer is still too short with failure to compare all three sources. 2–4 marks.

4. Look at **ALL** the sources. Which do you think gives the most useful evidence concerning the effects of the Black Death in England? (8)

Level 1 answer	Comments
Source **A** says that lots of men and women died and that their bodies were thrown into mass graves which stank after a time.	This answer makes a simple statement on a single source without further comment. 1–3 marks. If the answer had mentioned more than one source (even without comment) it should receive more marks.

Level 2 answer	Comments
C shows people abandoning their villages with their animals. **C** even suggests the medieval lack of understanding about how infectious the disease was. The lady does not seem to be afraid to be near the man covered in spots who must have the plague. Although the details of this source need to be treated with care, **C** offers much useful evidence concerning the effects of the plague. **B** gives useful information about the effects of different plague symptoms such as boils, spots and the coughing up of blood. The author is a modern historian who will have done careful research to ensure that what he says is accurate. He will have access to modern medical knowledge. Thus this source is both useful and reliable.	This is a top-of-the band answer at this level. The content and provenance of more than one source are analysed precisely with critical discussion of the material. 6–7 marks. An answer recognising that different sources may be used for different purposes, but consisting of only generalised comments with no exact analysis of content and provenance, might gain 4–5 marks at the lower end of this band.

Essays

Each part of an essay is assessed at level 1, level 2 or level 3. All the suggested essay answers in this book have been written as examples of the highest level. That is to say, level 3.

However, examples of the lower levels for one essay are offered here. The essay title on *The Battle of Hastings* may be found on page 68 of the pupils' book. A suggested answer at the top level appears in this book on pages 21–22. This should be compared with what follows. In the real examination, this essay would of course be written out in full sentences, as with all the other examples in this book. Poor writing style and weak spelling would play their part in helping an examiner to decide on a particular level.

(a)   Describe the main events of the Battle of Hastings.   (20)

Level 1 answer	Comments
• *The Battle of Hastings took place in 1066.* • *It was between the Normans and the English.* • *William was born in Normandy.* • *William's grandfather was a tanner.* • *Both William and Harold were very brave soldiers.* • *Bishop Odo fought in this battle.* • *An important tapestry gives a good idea of what went on and many old writers described it.* • *William encouraged his men by pushing off his helmet and shouting, 'Look, I am OK!'* • *The Norman archers fired lots of arrows at the English.* • *In the end, the English ran away.* • *Harold was hit in the eye and the Normans won.*	This answer is weak with poor recall of knowledge. There are some simple statements but a lack of detail. Much has been left out. Some material is irrelevant to the question. The material lacks structure. 1–8 marks.

Level 2 answer	Comments
• *The Battle of Hastings was fought in October 1066. Harold took up his position on Senlac Hill. William arranged his army in a valley.* • *Some Bretons helped him.* • *The Normans had archers, foot-soldiers and knights.* • *The Saxons made a shield-wall and had two-handed axes.* • *Lots of fighting then took place and Norman knights tried to break the Saxon battle line, but failed.* • *There was a rumour that William had been killed, so he encouraged his men by pushing back his helmet and shouting that he was still alive.* • *Many Saxon warriors rushed down the hill and were slaughtered by the Norman knights.* • *Harold was killed with an arrow.* • *William ordered his archers to fire their arrows onto the English.* • *In the end, the Saxons were chased from the battlefield.*	This answer contains more developed statements of fact and some relevant knowledge. However, key points are omitted and the sequence of events is uncertain. 9–15 marks.

(b) Explain how William I gained control over his new kingdom. (10)

Level 1 answer	Comments
• *William made a big book which told him how much land he had and how many people were in his kingdom.* • *He built lots of castles. These were called motte-and-bailey castles and soldiers lived in them.* • *William made a system called the feudal system where everybody had a lord.*	Three points are made here, but these simple statements are not developed and there is no attempt to use the material to answer the question. Much is left out. 1–4 marks.

Level 2 answer	Comments
● *William used castles to control his kingdom. At first these were wooden motte-and bailey types, but later, stone keeps appeared.* ● *The feudal system was tightened which helped William to keep command over his knights and peasants.* ● *William crushed rebellions. He beat Hereward the Wake in East Anglia after 1071.*	Three points are made with some coherent judgements. This time the analysis is developed. The significance of the facts is stated and related to the demands of the question. However, some key points are omitted. 5–8 marks.

Finally, I repeat what I have said before. Above everything else, enjoy what you write and let that sparkle come through your script. After all, you have chosen to tackle that particular essay.

Good luck!

Gavin Hannah
Oxford
Spring 2009

Answers to Evidence Questions

A. Medieval Realms: Britain 1066–1485

The First Crusade

1. The Crusaders climbed into Jerusalem using scaling ladders. (2)

2. First, the writer explains that the knights and the foot-soldiers had weapons such as swords and poleaxes. Secondly, he describes the Turks as 'unarmed'. (3)

3. Source **C** portrays exhausted and victorious Crusaders entering the city. This ties in with **A**, which mentions the Christian victory after so much suffering, and **B**, which describes the Christians in Jerusalem. **C** illustrates a mosque, which is mentioned in **A**. **C** also demonstrates the slaughter with dead bodies everywhere as mentioned in both **A** and **B**. **C** also shows weapons, like swords, as referred to in **B**. In these ways **C** supports **A** and **B**.

    However, **C** does not show the deaths of children, as described in **A** and **B**. In **C** there are also wounded horses and crosses on Crusader clothes, neither of which occurs in **A** or **B**. Source **C** thus only partly supports Sources **A** and **B**. (7)

4. All the sources have their use concerning the massacre at Jerusalem. As a 19th-century picture, **C** will not be accurate in its details. Its use is to give us an impression of what the massacre might have been like.

    B, on the other hand, offers us a medieval view. Although the writer is biased against his enemies, his bias is useful in illustrating the Christian opinion of the Turks at the time. 'Our men had the greatest hatred' for them, William wrote. His account of the massacre may be exaggerated and, as he was not present, his description must be treated with care.

    Perhaps the most useful and reliable is Source **A**, where a modern scholar has made careful research trying to get his facts correct. On the other hand, it should be remembered that he will have used sources such as **B** and **C** to make up his account. (8)

Matilda and Stephen

1. Stephen had a larger number of men than Geoffrey. (2)

2. Stephen was backed for the throne as the grandson of William the Conqueror. As a man, he was supported by those wishing to keep out Matilda because they did not want a woman ruler. (3)

3. **C** illustrates the precise relationship between the main characters in the story. We can see that Matilda is Henry I's daughter and that she is married to Geoffrey of Anjou as mentioned in **A**. The 'succession', discussed in **B**, is shown visually in **C** using a family tree. **C** therefore makes **B** easier to follow and understand. Matilda's position as heir is clear from this. It can be seen, too, that Stephen of Blois is Matilda's cousin. **C** offers a visual

statement of everyone's relative position, so that we may see exactly who was who and appreciate better their respective claims to the throne as outlined in **A** and **B**. (7)

4.   Although **C** accurately shows the leading royal relationships, its use is limited. **C** does not explain their motives or their relative strengths and weaknesses, nor why there should be war. Source **A** offers the evidence of a contemporary writer who may have understood the situation. Indeed, **A** gives us some precise reasons for the outbreak of war: Geoffrey was Stephen's sworn enemy; Matilda had been promised support to gain the crown; Stephen gathered men and money frustrating the wishes of Geoffrey and Matilda. The Chronicle does not appear to be biased, but we are unsure of its accuracy. It was also finished nearly 20 years after the events it describes. On the other hand, **B**, written by modern authors whose research should be exact, describes motives suggesting potential conflict. Matilda's succession has been recognised by the barons and Stephen is also strong with lands and has support from the barons. Thus, in terms of its content and reliability, it may be argued that **B** offers the most useful evidence for the cause of the civil war. (8)

Richard the Lionheart

1.   One of Richard's greatest achievements was to capture Cyprus in only a few weeks. (2)

2.   Richard inspired his men by being carried to fight among them and led them even though he was ill. He also showed great skill with his crossbow which would spur on his soldiers. (3)

3.   Source **C** shows Richard fighting with courage and determination. It demonstrates that he was a first-class warrior. This view is supported by his conquests and his military skills, as noted in **A**. His bravery, illustrated in **C**, would surely win the admiration of his commanders as mentioned in **A**. **C** and **B** both portray Richard as a man of action and as a skilful fighter. He is keen to get to grips with the enemy and puts his fighting duty before personal safety or comfort. Thus, **C** strongly supports the information given in **A** and **B**. (7)

4.   All the sources play their part in providing evidence about Richard's greatness on the battlefield. From **B**, we learn that he was a skilful tactician when besieging cities. His determination and fighting abilities are also mentioned. This information needs to be treated with care, as we do not know how Geoffrey acquired his facts. The author also seems to be biased in Richard's favour, so he may have exaggerated his good qualities.

Source **C** shows Richard as an action-man, fighting bravely. However, it is an imaginary, modern illustration. Although its overall impression is useful in suggesting the kind of man Richard was, its use is limited by being unrealistic in its details.

The most useful source is **A**. It provides details of some of Richard's battlefield achievements, which suggest his military greatness. This information should be accurate having been researched by a modern author. (8)

King John

1. King John sent messengers to his barons because he was frightened in case they attacked his castles. (2)

2. John was a good ruler because he used talented ministers who served him well. He also carried out many important policies, such as the development of trade. (3)

3. Source **C** shows John being forced by his barons to sign the *Magna Carta* in 1215. This agrees totally with **A**, which describes how this event had come about. **C** and **A** suggest that John was a poor ruler, as he was made to sign this agreement with his angry barons. These two sources support one another.

   On the other hand, **B** indicates that John was a good king. Had his barons agreed, there would have been no *Magna Carta* signing as illustrated in **C**. So, **C** does not support **B** at all. (7)

4. Source **B** is not the least useful in giving evidence for John as a ruler. It gives us lots of information, which should be reliable if the modern writer has researched carefully to find the truth. Source **A** is also not the least useful. What Roger says, however, should be treated with care. He was someone who appeared to favour the barons, as he mentions their 'joy' when John agreed to meet them. Also, his facts may be based on hearsay. As a monk, he was a churchman and John had offended the Church. However, we can still learn much concerning John's rule. He had obviously upset his barons and appears to be afraid of them.

   Perhaps the least useful source is **C**. It was produced long after 1215 and the details of the picture may be unreliable. Although we can see something being signed, the source (apart from the title) gives no details concerning John's rule. (8)

Edward I, Wales and Scotland

1. Edward I tried to beat the Scots by sending a series of large, well-equipped armies to invade them. (2)

2. The author's language suggests his hatred of Wallace. He is described as a robber, an arsonist and a murderer. Secondly, Wallace is compared to Herod, who was a very cruel king. The author believes Wallace was even worse. (3)

3. Source **C** shows Wallace being dragged to the gallows to be hanged. It also illustrates the axe which will be used to chop him up. **B** mentions the gallows, Wallace being dragged through the streets and his body being chopped into four parts. To this extent, **C** supports **B**. However, **B** then gives even fuller details of the execution.

   Source **A** describes Wallace's execution as 'brutal', and this brutality is shown in the picture in **C**. So there is a link between **C** and **A**. Overall, the picture in **C** gives more information than **A** about the execution but less than the description in **B**. **C** thus only partially supports these sources. (7)

4. Source **C** illustrates Edward's toughness on the Scots and shows what happened to his enemies. To this extent its general message is useful. However, as an imaginary, modern illustration, its details have only limited value.

    Source **B** also shows Edward's brutality towards his Scottish enemies. It describes Wallace's death in great detail. However, the English author is biased, so **B** needs to be treated with care. Nonetheless, this bias remains useful as an illustration of contemporary anti-Scottish feelings.

    Source **A** offers a range of useful information about the number and size of the campaigns. We can also see Edward's hatred of the Scots through the manner of Wallace's execution. This information should be reliable as it is the result of a historian's research. Thus, Source **A** is probably the most useful concerning Edward I's policy towards the Scots.   (8)

Edward II and Scotland

1. They ran away because they could not reach the Scots and were doing nothing in the battle.   (2)

2. Edward failed to make the best use of his archers by keeping them in the rear. He also left before the battle was finished causing his army to give up and run away.   (3)

3. Source **C** shows the English knights unsuccessfully attacking the Scottish pikemen. This agrees with **A**, which describes a similar scene as the English horses 'rushed on to the Scottish pikes, which bristled like a dense forest'. Mortally wounded horses and the English failure to break the Scots feature both in **C** and **A**.

    Although **B** and **C** agree that the English failed, **B** provides reasons for the English defeat which are not concerned with the failure of the knights. **C** agrees more with **A** in explaining why the English were unable to win, owing to their inability to break the Scottish battle line.   (7)

4. Source **C** gives a clear idea of the struggle between the English knights and the Scottish pikemen. Although useful for a general impression of the fighting, its value is limited. First, it shows only a tiny part of the battle. Secondly, as a modern, imaginary drawing, its detail cannot be reliable.

    Source **A** offers a broader view of events with some interesting details of the actual sounds during the conflict as pikes splintered and horses screamed in agony. Despite being a contemporary source, its material is second hand. We cannot be sure just how 'trustworthy' the eyewitness was.

    The details of the battle in **B** should be accurate. This is modern writing based on careful research. The title of the book *Military Blunders* and expressions like 'dubious achievement' suggest that Edward II should have won. **B** thus presents a judgement on the battle, as well as information about it. As such, it is perhaps the most useful source.   (8)

The Black Death 1348–1350

1. Families had to bury their dead because, as so many people had died, there was a
    shortage of grave-diggers.   (2)

2. Some victims had boils and could survive if these were cut out. Others had small black
    spots of puss all over their bodies and usually died.   (3)

3. Source **C** shows a man with spots all over his body and this agrees with what is said
    about 'black spots' in **B**. **C** also illustrates burning houses and people fleeing from their
    village, neither of which is mentioned in either **A** or **B**. **C** does not portray any burial
    details, nor does it refer to the high number of deaths, both of which are discussed in **A**.
    Overall, the illustration in **C** does not agree with the description in **A** at all and only
    partly supports the extract in **B**.   (7)

4. All the sources are useful for showing the effects of the plague. **A** describes the shortage
    of labour and the high death rate. The writer might have been an eyewitness. There is no
    reason to doubt the accuracy of his account, especially as it is thought that about one
    third of the population perished.

    B gives useful information concerning the effects of the different symptoms. As the writer
    of this source has access to modern medical knowledge, his information is both useful and
    accurate.

    C, too, offers much evidence concerning the effects of the plague. We note that it caused
    people to burn their houses and abandon their plague villages with their animals. **C** even
    suggests the medieval lack of understanding about how infectious the disease was. The
    lady does not seem to be afraid to be near the man covered in spots who must have the
    plague. Although the details of this source need to be treated with care, **C** is perhaps the
    most useful for describing the actual effects of the plague.   (8)

Henry V

1. The first attack came against the English front from the two ends of the French
    battle line.   (2)

2. The French leadership was weakened by divisions, jealousies and over-confidence.
    Experienced and important commanders had to follow the wishes of royal princes.
    The French were also unable to carry out their potentially winning battle plan.   (3)

3. Source **C** illustrates the English archers, protected by stakes, cutting down French knights
    with their arrows. This agrees closely with **A**, which says that the French failed to win as
    their knights were forced to retreat because of the arrows and the stakes. Source **B**
    stresses the ineffectual French command system. It makes no reference to what is shown
    in **C**, with its failed cavalry attacks, archers and stakes. Thus, **C** agrees more with **A**.   (7)

4. Source **A** offers an account of some events during the battle. As contemporary,
    eyewitness evidence, it is valuable. However, it needs to be read with care. Thomas

Elmham, writing about his king, through bias, may have exaggerated his successes at Agincourt. Nonetheless, **A** remains useful for information on fighting techniques.

Source **C** is an imaginary, modern picture. It may even be based on earlier sources such as **A**. Although of use in providing an impression of the battle, its details are unreliable.

Source **B**, produced by modern historians, offers a reliable, partial explanation for the French defeat. However, it concentrates on leadership issues. It does not give any battle details. Reading it leaves us in the dark about the precise events of the conflict. Thus, it ranks as the least useful source for telling us what actually happened during the Battle of Agincourt. (8)

Women in Medieval Society

1. One task was to spin wool. (2)

2. The writer believes that women should understand, and be able to deal with, accounts. They should also know how to hire good labourers and how to supervise them carefully. (3)

3. Source **C** illustrates women spinning and carding wool, tasks which are also referred to in **A**. There is no mention of washing wool or of wages in **C**. Thus, **C** only partly supports **A** concerning women's duties.

   Source **C** does not support **B** at all. The information in **B** is totally different from that in the illustration in **C**. **B** outlines duties for the rich; **C** shows the jobs of the poor. The only point of agreement is that both sources refer to tasks performed by women and that women doing their jobs properly would be busy. (7)

4. All the sources are useful in building a picture of women's duties. Source **C** illustrates exactly what spinning and carding were like in medieval times. **C** is useful too in telling us that these jobs were carried out by women. It is an illustration of a scene from medieval life made on a larger document, as we can see from the Latin writing, and there is no reason to doubt its accuracy.

   Source **A** is also valuable. We are told about the work of poorer women and are provided with useful material concerning wages and the organisation of the textile industry through merchants. **A** should be reliable and exact if the historian has researched carefully.

   Source **B** gives us a mass of material. It is a contemporary view and is useful in telling us what should be done ideally by noble women. To this extent, it is valuable. However, it may not represent what happened in reality and this limits its reliability.

   Overall, **A** provides the best view of women's duties, both in terms of what it says and its reliability. (8)

B. The Making of the United Kingdom: 1485–1750

Henry VII

1. Henry was not warlike. He is described as 'preferring peace to war'. (2)

2. Henry believed wealth would make him strong, giving him the means of crushing the over-mighty nobles. He also thought that money strengthened the whole image of his kingship. (3)

3. Source **C** suggests that Henry was careful with money and that he thoroughly checked all his accounts. His initials are placed at the bottom of the page. This supports **B** in showing Henry's belief in the importance of money. Because Henry valued wealth, he was careful when handling it. **C** records the reasons for Henry's payments, suggesting a 'wise and prudent' character as noted in **A**.

   C also supports **A**, where we learn that Henry became a miser in his 'later days'. Misers scrutinise their accounts, watching every penny, as Henry does in **C**, noting all the outgoings from his treasury. (7)

4. Source **A** is useful, giving us a contemporary opinion on avarice in a ruler and its bad effects on the kingdom. The importance of money is implied through the concerns over its misuse. Vergil seems to be a reliable writer. He knew Henry VII and has spoken to those close to the king. His observations are probably true.

   B provides valuable evidence of the general political and military uses of wealth. Henry VII needed to be strong and money formed an important part of the creation and maintenance of his power. The author of a historical dictionary would try his best to be accurate, so this information is reliable.

   C is an official source revealing the importance of money specifically to Henry VII. Henry's initials suggest that the material is accurate as the king has checked and approved it.

   Perhaps **B** is the most useful source in the sense that it makes the most general comments about the importance of money. (8)

Henry VIII

1. By 1547, England was poor on account of Henry's expensive wars. (2)

2. Henry gave England a greater sense of independence and identity by smashing the power of the Pope. Secondly, he increased England's reputation abroad so that she could take her place among the great European powers. (3)

3. Both **C** and **A** agree that Henry had successfully challenged papal authority. **C** shows Henry in his classic pose, legs apart and hands on hips, suggesting power, confidence and success. This reflects the comments in **A** that he crushed his enemies, made great changes within his kingdom and cast a long shadow over English history. **C** makes no reference to Henry's wars, as in **A**.

B and C agree on Henry's defeat of the Pope. The writing on the tablet in **C** praises Henry for being greater than his father. This is reflected in **B**, where Henry has established England as a power to rival France and the Empire, as well as laying strong foundations for Elizabeth I. On balance, **C** agrees in many ways, directly and implied, with both **A** and **B**. (7)

4. Source **A**, reliable evidence by a modern writer seeking historical truth, provides a wealth of information concerning Henry's specific achievements. There are also aspects of his character suggesting a ruthless and successful man of action. Likewise **B**, another modern, reliable source, presents a range of long- and short-term successes both at home and abroad.

   Source **C** is more difficult to interpret. Apart from the text on the tablet, the viewer is left to put his own interpretation on the picture. Such opinions, although interesting, even when deduced from the source, may be inaccurate. The text is vague concerning Henry's precise achievements. The inscription may be exaggerated. Holbein worked for Henry. He would therefore avoid criticism and only lavish praise on the king. On this basis, it may be argued that **C** is the least useful source for an assessment of Henry's reign. (8)

Henry VIII and his Great Matter

1. The picture suggests that Catherine was shocked and angry. (2)

2. Henry wanted to divorce Catherine because she was past child-bearing age and he needed a son to rule after him. Secondly, Anne Boleyn was pregnant and Henry loved her and wanted her as his wife. (3)

3. Source **B** is the final judgement of Cranmer's court, which is then shown being passed on to Catherine in the picture in **C**. Sources **B** and **A** agree about the important part played by Cranmer during the divorce process. **B** mentions the fact that Cranmer 'inspected the opinions of legal experts', which supports what is said in **A** about him consulting foreign scholars. The whole of **B** forms the verdict of Cranmer's court, referred to in **A**. In these ways **B** supports both the description in **A** and the picture in **C**.

   On the other hand, there is no mention in **B** of the actual reasons for the divorce, which are provided in Source **A**. (7)

4. Source **C** shows Catherine's feelings on receiving the news of her divorce, but, as a 19th-century picture painted long after the event, it is unlikely to be accurate. Also, it does not tell us how the divorce was obtained.

   Source **B** is valuable. It can be trusted as an official document and it reveals that a lot of care was taken by Cranmer to obtain the best legal advice during the long divorce process. Source **A** offers a great deal of information concerning the causes of the divorce and it also reveals what Cranmer did. We learn that much care was taken to consult a wide range of expert opinion in foreign countries. This is a dependable source, as a modern historian will have done his research in order to be as truthful as he can.

   Overall, Source **A** provides the most useful evidence, both in terms of the information it gives and because of its reliability. (8)

Lady Jane Grey and Mary I

1. People did not like the idea of Jane Grey as queen. There were no celebrations and few said, 'God save her'. (2)

2. Northumberland persuaded Edward VI to change his will, excluding Mary and leaving the crown to Lady Jane Grey's children. When it became obvious that this scheme would fail, Northumberland had the will altered again. This time Jane Grey herself was to inherit the crown. Once more Mary was left out. (3)

3. Source **C** illustrates Mary's entry into London. Lots of ordinary people have turned out to cheer her. They appear joyful, as do the men on their knees, receiving the queen. Mary is warmly welcomed by all classes.

    C supports **A** in describing the celebrations after Mary's proclamation as queen. **B** reveals the initial arrangements for Mary to become queen after Edward VI if he died childless. It was only Northumberland's wild scheme which overturned this. Most people regarded Mary as the rightful ruler. Jane Grey received little popular support as shown in **A**. Overall, **C** is perhaps closer to **A** than **B**. They each illustrate whom most people wanted as monarch and their pleasure at Mary's accession. (7)

4. Source **C** illustrates the result of the succession struggle. Mary is crowned. **C** presents that historical truth. However, its utility is limited. As a modern, imaginary picture, its details are unreliable. Source **A**, in describing two queens, implies that there had been a power struggle, though it offers no details. We learn what contemporaries thought about the relative popularity of the candidates. Although the chronicle would seem to be accurate, we should perhaps allow for some bias against Jane Grey.

    The most useful source is **B**. It describes exactly how Henry VIII had arranged the succession and how his plans were systematically set aside by Northumberland as the situation unfolded. Writing a modern textbook, the author will try to be accurate. Thus, both in terms of content and reliability, **B** offers the student the best account of the struggle for the crown in 1553. (8)

Mary I and the Protestants

1. Cranmer put his hand into the fire. (2)

2. Cranmer's strong Protestant beliefs are shown as follows: he ignored Friar John who was trying to make him Roman Catholic again and he looked up to Heaven asking Jesus to take his spirit. (3)

3. Source **C** supports Sources **A** and **B** in several ways. **C** shows us that the martyrs were executed by burning, which is mentioned in both **A** and **B**. The method of burning using faggots, shown in **C**, agrees with **B** where wood was kindled. In **C**, the martyrs look brave. Bravery and courage are again reflected in both **A** and **B**. The main difference is that **C** depicts a multiple execution, while in **A** and **B** only one person is at the stake. (7)

4. All the sources are useful concerning Mary's treatment of Protestants. Each shows that Protestants were treated harshly and faced a painful death. The sources reveal that people of all kinds were burned. **A** and **B** talk about bishops and Archbishop Cranmer, while **C** depicts the execution of ordinary people. That all classes died suggests that Mary was passionate about her Roman Catholic faith. The sources also reveal that, despite Mary's cruelty, Protestants died bravely. However, **B** is from a book published later, in the reign of Elizabeth I, which was meant to glorify the martyrs, so it may be biased in their favour. Its content should be treated with care. **C** was produced long after the event and, although it illustrates generally what happened at an execution, it may not be accurate in its detail. Again, this source must be used with caution. However, the modern writer of **A** would try to be accurate, based upon his research, so this source is perhaps the most useful owing to its reliability.   (8)

Elizabeth I

1. Elizabeth's bad moods are like a sudden thunderstorm.   (2)

2. Elizabeth's queenly importance is stressed through the artist's attention to the details of her dress and her jewels. Secondly, her political importance is shown by the Tudor Rose and the Fleur de Lys, each under a crown, signifying her rule over England and her claim to the French throne.   (3)

3. Source **B** states that Elizabeth was always 'ornately dressed with a profusion of jewels'. This is clearly shown in **C**. Her dress is covered with pearls, diamonds and rubies, together with the pelican pendant on her chest. Elizabeth's image of 'majesty', as mentioned in **B**, is illustrated by **C**. The portrait suggests power, confidence and regal authority. Elizabeth's ability to frighten people, as described in **B**, agrees with **A** concerning her mood swings and her temper tantrums. Neither the comment in **A** nor the portrait in **C**, refers to her learning or to her artistic tastes, as touched on in **B**.   (7)

4. Source **A** presents a simple, honest opinion of Elizabeth's character written by a contemporary eyewitness who knew the queen. Hatton had no apparent grievance against Elizabeth so there is no reason to doubt the truth of his assessment.

    Source **B** describes several aspects of the queen's character such as her manners, her learning and her dislike of art and literature. This information, from a modern writer based on careful research, should be accurate.

    C, on the other hand, is a portrait painted for propaganda purposes. It was specifically meant to send particular messages to her people; in this case, royal power and love for her subjects. Despite outward appearances, with all the finery and artistic beauty, the real Elizabeth may have been a totally different person. It may be argued that the queen's true character was smothered by art and that the painting depicts how she wanted to be seen rather than how she genuinely was. On this basis, **C** offers little to the student of Elizabeth's character.   (8)

The Causes of the Civil War 1629–1641

1. They decided to use a Bill of Attainder because Strafford could simply be declared guilty without any proof. (2)

2. Pym claimed that Strafford had committed treason against God by betraying his truth. He had weakened the power and glory of the king and he had destroyed England's prosperity. (3)

3. Source **C** shows huge crowds which had come to watch Strafford's execution. The size of the crowd suggests that many people did not like him and wanted him dead. This supports the evidence of **A**, where the London mob rioted when they thought Strafford might be let off any punishment. Strafford's unpopularity is again shown in **B**, where serious charges are made by Pym covering wide areas of treason. Pym hated Strafford and did all he could to have him executed. Thus, **C** fully supports the idea of Strafford's unpopularity, which is hinted at in **A** and **B**. (7)

4. Source **C** provides the least useful evidence of why Strafford was executed. Although it is a useful contemporary source giving a clear image of Strafford's death, it does not mention why the execution took place. On the other hand, **A** and **B** are totally concerned with the reasons for Strafford's death. **A** mentions that he was accused of treason, that he was unpopular and that Charles I was forced to sacrifice him. As a modern source, it should be accurate if the author has been careful with his research.

    Source **B**, although biased against Strafford, again provides clear reasons why his enemies thought that he should die. It is only in **C** where the actual causes of Strafford's death are not mentioned. Thus, **C** is the least useful source when trying to explain exactly why Strafford went to the block. (8)

The Battle of Marston Moor

1. As the source says that Oliver Cromwell was wounded, he is the man in the centre of the picture with his arm in a sling. (2)

2. God disliked the Parliamentarians because they had rebelled against their anointed king. Likewise, He disapproved of the Royalists' overconfidence, which allowed victory to slip from their grasp. (3)

3. Source **C** speaks of heavy Royalist losses. This would seem to agree with **A**, where Cromwell and his Parliamentarians are causing Royalist casualties with their cavalry charge. There is a measure of agreement, too, between **B** and **C** over the fact that the Royalists allowed Parliament to snatch victory from the jaws of defeat. On the other hand, **B** contradicts **C** in claiming that more Parliamentarians were killed. **C** refers to 'an unusually large number of casualties' on both sides, whereas **B** states that 'so few' died in the battle. On this basis, **C** agrees mostly with **A**. (7)

4. Source **C**, from a modern book, written after careful research, should provide accurate information. We learn that Marston Moor was a bloody battle with a high number of

casualties and that the Parliamentary army snatched an unexpected military success. **C**, though, does not reveal many details of what actually happened during the battle.

B suggests that not many men were killed overall, then comments on the relative number of casualties and prisoners between the two sides. It also suggests that the Royalists allowed victory to slip through their fingers. The information comes from a contemporary eyewitness, but it is a Royalist source and, as such, must be interpreted with care, allowing for bias. Again, specific battle details are lacking.

A, on the other hand, shows a battle scene. We note the cavalry charge led by Cromwell and that it was decisive in helping to bring victory to Parliament. Even though the precise details from a 19th-century history book are unlikely to be accurate, this source offers more information than the others concerning the actual events during the battle.   (8)

The Plague of London 1665

1.   There was not time to bury the bodies properly because lots of people died so quickly.   (2)

2.   Pepys noted the streets were empty of healthy people, but full of those sick with the plague. He noticed that everybody was talking about the plague.   (3)

3.   Source **C** illustrates plague victims being buried in a large, single grave. This supports what is said in **A** about bodies not being buried properly. **C** also depicts a man with a cart ringing a hand-bell, which further agrees with what is described in **A**. There is no real agreement between **C** and **B**, other than the fact that people were dying. **B** describes the conditions in town, whereas **C** shows a scene outside the city. There are people praying in **C**. This is not mentioned in either **A** or **B**. Thus, although there is some agreement, **C** only partially supports the information given in **A** and hardly matches what is said in **B**. (7)

4.   All the sources add to our knowledge of the plague. **C** illustrates the death-cart and the burial of bodies in sheets not coffins. The people praying suggest that many asked God for help during this disaster. On the other hand, the details of the picture are not accurate which limits its use. **B** is an eyewitness account, revealing a lot of information about streets and conversations. This is valuable. We get some idea of how people felt, which is often hard to record in history. Pepys himself seems sad. There is no reason to doubt the accuracy of what he writes. Source **A** provides information on the numbers of plague deaths, the state of the streets, the agonies of the illness and details of burials. It is reliable as the author would have researched carefully before writing his account. **A** is perhaps the most reliable of the three sources and, as such, is the most useful to someone studying the London Plague of 1665.   (8)

James II and the Glorious Revolution

1.   One sign of welcome was that the English raised their hats to William.   (2)

2.   James promised to co-operate with his people to respect their liberties and the freedom of the Church of England.   (3)

3. Source **B** assures William that the majority of people will support him as they want a change of king. The English are tired of government under James II. This attitude is reflected in **C** showing William receiving a warm welcome on his arrival in England. **B** bears little relation to **A** which contains no evidence of English attitudes to William. **A** describes James II's intentions in 1685. The extract in Source **B** thus supports the illustration in **C**, but not the description in **A**. (7)

4. All the sources are useful in helping us build up a picture of why William III became king of England. Source **A** sets out what James II said he would do. He failed to keep his promises, hence the need for William. As **A** is from a modern book, what it says should be reliable. The author will have tried to be accurate. **C** suggests that William became king because he had lots of English support. However, it is a picture produced long after 1688 and we should treat its details with care. Nonetheless, it is probably accurate in showing an overall welcoming attitude. Source **B**, written at the time of the Revolution by people who witnessed the events, offers clear evidence about why William was wanted. James II had governed badly and was getting worse. The only solution was to seek a new monarch. Source **B** was produced by James's enemies so it might make his reign sound worse than it was. **B** is biased towards William III. However, of the three sources it offers, perhaps, the best evidence of contemporary English attitudes towards James II and thus of why William III took the throne. (8)

The Jacobite Rebellion of 1745

1. Cope was defeated mainly because of the success of the Highland Charge. (2)

2. After a short prayer, the Highlanders advanced, fired their muskets, threw them down, drew their swords and rushed upon the enemy shouting their war-cries. (3)

3. Source **C** shows the Highlanders charging forward with their swords and shields. In one sense, **C** does not support **A** or **B** at all, because there is no evidence of muskets. Only swords and bill-hooks are illustrated. On the other hand, if **C** is taken to represent a later stage in the charge, then it fully supports the information given in **A** and **B** by showing the Jacobites rushing upon their enemies in an attempt to drive them from the battlefield. (7)

4. All the sources are useful in helping to build a full picture of the Highland Charge at Prestonpans. At first sight, **B** seems to be the most useful. It was written by an eyewitness and it provides a lot of detail. However, it is a Jacobite account so it may be biased. It may overestimate the success of the charge.

    Source **C** was produced long after the event and presents an ideal view of the Highland Charge. It is useful for giving an overall visual impression of what might have happened, but needs to be treated with caution as its details are unlikely to be correct.

    Source **A** offers the balanced account of a modern historian who has completed his research, trying to be accurate and find the truth. Even this author, though, relies on John Home's evidence, which may not be exact. Nonetheless, with this limitation in mind, **A** perhaps provides the most useful and reliable evidence as to what happened during the Highland Charge at Prestonpans. (8)

C. Britain: 1750–circa 1900

The French Revolution

1. Source **A** mentions the radicals who followed the revolutionaries in believing that the monarchy was unfair and that there should be greater equality in Britain. (2)

2. The Englishman was angry because the king and the British people had been insulted. Secondly, he hated the idea of any foreign authority meddling in British affairs, trying to import greater freedoms to London. (3)

3. Source **C** depicts French liberty, with rebellion, murder, atheism and private ruin, as bringing misery. British liberty, with religion, law and order and prosperity, generated happiness. **C** is anti-French. This is echoed in **B**, where the English gentleman whips and throws out the foreigner for suggesting that French revolutionary ideas could liberate Englishmen from tyranny. On the other hand, **A** suggests that, despite some opposition, many people in Britain believed that greater freedom and equality were needed. These viewed the French Revolution favourably. Thus, **C** mostly disagrees with **A**. (7)

4. Source **A** is informative, providing much information about British views of the French Revolution. We learn about the radicals and their ideas supporting those of the French reformers. We note, too, that some British people opposed the Revolution. This material, based on modern research, should be accurate and reliable.

    C offers an anti-French view of the Revolution. Although the pamphlet was written by only one man, it must have been approved by others for it to merit publication. Thus, we may deduce that what is said reflects the opinions of many more people.

    On the other hand, **B**, although taking an anti-French stance, represents the actions and opinions of only one person. It describes a single, isolated incident. Its publication as an item of news in no way required widespread support. Its outlook is narrow. In this respect, **B** perhaps provides the least useful evidence concerning British views of the French Revolution. (8)

The Battle of Waterloo

1. The French cavalry could not break the British because many were killed by musket shots. (2)

2. When the French attacked, they suffered heavy losses. Also, the French cavalry retreated in confusion as the British squares held firm. (3)

3. Source **C** shows the British formed into squares with the French attacking, suffering huge losses and failing to break through. This agrees with the information given in **A** and **B** about the cavalry failing to penetrate the British lines. **C** also illustrates the display of gallant French horsemen and their uniforms, as mentioned in **B**. There is thus strong agreement between **C** and **B**. Source **C** shows only one of the attacks and so differs from

A, which tells us that the French charged several times. Despite this difference, **C** generally supports what is said in sources **A** and **B**. (7)

4. All the sources show that the British used muskets to deal with the French cavalry attacks. From **A** we may deduce that the British technique was effective as the French tried to break through several times and failed. Source **A** also offers reliable material based on the careful research of a modern historian. **B** is an English source and so may be biased against the French. However, it was written fairly soon after the battle and its description of exactly what took place during an attack would seem to be trustworthy. **C** is useful as it offers a visual image of the cavalry attacks so that a historian may get some idea of the confusion and excitement of battle and of how the squares worked when dealing with attacking horsemen. However, the details of the picture cannot be accurate and this needs to be kept in mind when using this evidence.

When considered with care, all the sources contribute to our understanding of the English reaction to French cavalry attacks. (8)

The Great Reform Bill of 1832

1. The rioters set fire to property. (2)

2. Macaulay says that the lower orders sometimes suffered because they were poor. They also became angry when 'their passions' were inflamed. It was anger and poverty which made them riot in support of reform. (3)

3. Source **C** shows rioting, looting and buildings being destroyed and burnt. There are also some troops present to keep order. All these ideas feature in **A**, so there is strong support between **C** and **A**, even though **C** does not illustrate any deaths or wounding. On the other hand, **C** does not directly support **B** at all. Although **B** mentions angry men being eager to relieve their suffering, which could lead to violence, there is no mention of any actual rioting. (7)

4. **C** offers an image of the riots. This is a useful way to present information, a picture often being worth more than lots of words. But even though this source dates from the 19th century and gives a good impression of what took place, its details cannot be trusted. This limits its usefulness. **B** is an honest and accurate source, giving us the personal views of an upper-class contemporary. It is thus helpful in telling us how people of the time, in Macaulay's position, viewed the causes of the rioting. **B** is also useful as it shows us exactly why some of the rioting occurred. Source **A** provides precise features of the riots in various cities, telling us that there was widespread violence and that government troops were brought in to restore order. As a modern source, based upon thorough research, **A** should be both trustworthy and accurate.

Thus, in terms of its content and reliability, **A** perhaps provides the most useful evidence about the Reform Bill riots. (8)

Chartism

1. The House of Commons always refused to hear the Petitions. The strength of their opposition was suggested when the First Petition was rejected by 235 votes to 46. (2)

2. Attwood championed the Chartists in two ways. First, he said that the movement was supported by over 214 towns and villages, together with important cities like Birmingham. Secondly, he claimed that the men who signed the petition were all hard-working, honest, law-abiding citizens. (3)

3. Source **C** shows Thomas Duncombe introducing the Second Petition to Parliament with over three million signatures. The Petition may be seen piled on the floor of the Commons. This suggests heavy support for Chartism. This is supported by **A**, which states that 'hundreds of thousands of people' signed the Petition. Further great support for Chartism, with over one-and-a-quarter million signatures, is illustrated by **B**. Source **C**, however, agrees mostly with **B**. **C** and **B** describe the large number of signatures and each refers to individual champions of Chartism introducing their opinions to the House of Commons. (7)

4. All the sources contribute to our understanding of Chartism. They suggest that the movement was well supported and a comparison of the figures from **B** and **C** shows that its influence was growing. All the sources demonstrate the methods used to press the Chartist demands. **B** tells us the kind of men the Chartists were. **A** suggests that Chartists were determined as they kept making new petitions. However, this source also implies that Chartism was a lost cause owing to the vast opposition from Parliament.

    Source **B** suggests that support was widespread. The general idea of support for Chartism is illustrated in **C**. However, the details of this image may be inaccurate. This limits its usefulness. **B** is biased towards the Chartists. As a supporter, Attwood was bound to claim that all Chartists were good men. He could have exaggerated their positive qualities, as well as the extent of their support. His material needs to be handled with caution, despite being a contemporary source.

    The extract in Source **A** perhaps offers the most useful evidence, both in terms of its content and reliability. (8)

The Crimean War

1. Tennyson says that 600 men took part in the charge. (2)

2. Lieutenant Phillips faced artillery fire from his left, his right and the front, from the guns at the bottom of the valley. There was also rifle fire from infantry to his right. (3)

3. Source **C** shows the charge in full swing with shot from the right, left and front. This supports both **A** and **B**. **C** also agrees with **A** and **B** in depicting the boldness and bravery of the men. **B** and **C** convey something of the pace of the charge, which is not remarked on in **A**. **C** and **B** also refer to the ground being 'strewed with men'. This is not mentioned in **A**. Owing to these differences, it may be argued that **C** mostly disagrees with **A** concerning the detail of the charge. (7)

4.	Source **C** gives a useful impression of the charge. Simpson visited the battlefield to check its geography and discussed his sketches with Cardigan who led the charge. However, despite this, the artist severely reduced the utility of this evidence by reducing the valley size in the interests of artistic licence to add excitement to his picture. He has tampered with the truth.

A provides general material about the charge. We learn where the canons were and that it was a brave attack. However, this evidence is fiction, if based on fact. Through its language: 'boldly they rode', 'jaws of Death' and 'mouth of Hell', the poem stresses heroism. This produces good literature but bad history.

The most useful source is **B**. It is an eyewitness account full of details concerning the speeds of the attack, the quality and direction of the fire and the manner in which men fell. Phillips took part in the charge and there is little reason to doubt what he wrote. Even allowing for memory lapses, this source offers much useful, precise evidence concerning the fate of the Light Brigade.						(8)

The Indian Mutiny

1.	The men were killed with pistols.						(2)

2.	The garrison surrendered because food supplies were running low and they believed that everyone would starve to death before the arrival of reinforcements. Also, Wheeler had received an offer of safe conduct and thus thought surrender would save lives.		(3)

3.	Source **C** shows the British punishing sepoy rebels by blowing them to bits. This is an example of British cruelty. On the other hand, Sources **A** and **B** describe Indian cruelty. **A** says that the rebels made fun of the British before shooting them. **B** again illustrates Indian cruelty and also deceit, as the rebel leader broke his promise of safe conduct for the garrison. Thus, there is no agreement between **C** and Sources **A** and **B**. **C** applies to the British and **A** and **B** to the rebels.						(7)

4.	All the sources play their part in building up a picture of the cruelties of the Indian Mutiny. **C** suggests that the British showed no mercy to the rebels once order had been restored, and depicts a savage method of execution.

Source **A** indicates cruelty, with innocent women and children being butchered and the men shot only after being mocked. There is horror, too, in **B** as the bodies of men and women, having been hacked to death with sabres and knives, are disrespectfully thrown down a well.

Although **A** was produced at the time, as a British source, it may be biased against the rebels, exaggerating their barbarity. Similarly, **C** may not be accurate in its details, although it conveys a general idea of how some rebels were punished. The information in **A** and **C** requires careful handling which limits their usefulness as sources.

B offers a lot of material based upon careful modern historical research. Therefore, in terms of its content and reliability, **B** perhaps provides the most useful evidence concerning the cruelties of the Mutiny.						(8)

The Cotton Industry

1. Children performed minor tasks because machinery had become too complicated for them to operate. (2)

2. When operating a mule, the main job was performed by the spinner who controlled the machine. There was also a piecer who repaired any broken threads. (3)

3. Source **C** illustrates adults operating spinning mules, while a child performs the simple job of sweeping up under the machine. This agrees with **A** about children carrying out only secondary tasks. **B** describes the work of various members of a mule team. Adults run the machines, while children perform minor tasks such as joining threads or sweeping, which is clearly shown in **C**. In these ways **C** fully agrees with the information provided in **A** and **B** about children doing inferior jobs. However, **C** also illustrates the construction of a spinning mill and shows how the machines were powered with drive-shafts, none of which is mentioned in either **A** or **B**. (7)

4. Source **C** shows clearly what some children did. However, the actual details of the picture may not be accurate. This limits its use even though the image dates from the 19th century. **B** is a description of the ideal method of working a spinning mule. It was written at the time and is likely to be an accurate statement of what children were generally expected to do. **A** is also useful. Not only does it describe the part played by children in mills, but it also explains why they had to perform such tasks. This information should be correct having been carefully researched by a modern historian. Thus, all the sources play their part in providing evidence of children's role in a cotton mill. However, in terms of content and reliability, **A** perhaps provides the most useful material. (8)

Trade Unions

1. Loveless wanted to form a union branch because the wages of farm labourers had been reduced. (2)

2. Some employers tried to get rid of unions by using lock-outs. Only if a worker agreed to leave his union could he regain his job. Secondly, the force of the law was used against unions, whose members risked transportation and ruin for their families. (3)

3. Source **C** does not mention anything about lock-outs or Robert Owen's GNCTU, which are considered in **B**. The main message of **C** is that anyone forming a union was committing a serious crime, the punishment for which was seven years' transportation if found guilty. This agrees with **A**, where the Tolpuddle Martyrs, having tried to set up a union, were sentenced to seven years' imprisonment in Tasmania. The warning to union members explained in **C**, affected peoples' attitudes and actions. This idea is supported in **B**. Many did not risk joining unions, fearing transportation. (7)

4. All the sources play their part in building up a picture of union problems. **C** makes the point that any union association was considered a serious crime, carrying a harsh penalty. **C** is an official notice, presenting a useful snapshot of a particular case. Its 'official' status makes it reliable evidence of the magistrates' intentions.

A, as a textbook, is helpful in offering accurate and reliable material concerning union problems. However, the source confines itself to one particular case which reduces its value when considering the wider picture.

B is another reliable source. The author should have researched carefully seeking historical truth. It takes a broad view. We note how union opponents tried to get rid of the unions, that Owen's union was short-lived and that the Tolpuddle Case had widespread effects, slowing union growth because of the difficulties it raised. On the basis of reliability and content, **B** may be regarded as the best source for evidence about the problems facing early trade unions. (8)

Slavery and the Triangular Trade

1. Traders took as many slaves as possible because they made a huge profit from each one they landed in the Americas. (2)

2. Slaves might die from being crushed to death as they were packed tightly together. They could also suffocate, as many of them were not able to have enough air. (3)

3. Source **C** shows large numbers of slaves carefully arranged so that as many as possible could be fitted on board. This helps us to understand the phrase in **A**, 'the slaves were packed as tightly as possible', by indicating exactly how this was managed.

   Source **C** likewise illustrates the cramming and packing of slaves, revealing how they were fitted into the low spaces between the decks and showing that many of them were shut out from light and air. This backs up what is said in **B**. Overall, **C** greatly helps us to understand **A** and **B** by providing us with a clear image of what is written in the other two sources. (7)

4. Source **A** provides us with much information about slaves on slave ships. What is said should be reliable if the historian has carried out thorough and accurate research. **B** also gives us a lot of data, including the fact that nearly 10% of the slaves died on this particular trip. It is a contemporary source and the trader is describing what he has seen. That this source is reliable is suggested by the author's apparent surprise that so many slaves could be fitted onto one ship. **C**, too, is reliable in showing the crammed conditions on a slave ship. The whole purpose of this diagram is to illustrate just how the maximum number of slaves could be theoretically squeezed into the available space.

   All these sources are useful both for the information they give and for their reliability. However, in terms of content and reliability, **B** perhaps provides the most useful contribution to our understanding of the conditions in which slaves were shipped to the Americas. It describes an actual case. (8)

The British Empire

1. The Egyptians formed a National Party with a slogan, 'Egypt for the Egyptians', to oppose British and French interference. (2)

2. The British Empire came about partly to expand trade, thus increasing the nation's wealth. The British government also annexed areas of strategic importance in order to expand its power. (3)

3. The message in **C** is that the British viewed their empire with confidence and pride. Imperial power was theirs by right. This agrees with the second part of **B**, which states that, by 1870, British enthusiasm for the Empire had become widespread. **A** opposes **C**, arguing that Britain has no automatic right to dominate other nations. Indeed, as it valued its own nationalism, Britain ought not to condemn the feelings of nationalism in others which British aggression might stimulate. (7)

4. Source **A** reflects the importance of the Empire with the move to protect British rights in Egypt. We note the imperial position was questioned by some, like the Workmen's Peace Association. **A** is biased to them, as the evidence comes from one of their meetings. Nonetheless, **A** is useful in providing an anti-imperial view. By showing the disagreements over the Empire, **A** suggests that it was an important issue for British people at the time.

   B offers much on imperialism. We learn that, over the 19th century, views changed. By the 1870s, the imperial idea was important even for ordinary people. For the government, the Empire represented a way to increase trade and strategic power. For the Church, it was a method of 'civilising' backward peoples. Presented in a history textbook, this material should be useful and accurate.

   C, as a *Punch* cartoon, is a reliable snapshot of imperial perceptions in 1882. Obviously, the Empire was important. However, **C** offers a narrow picture. There is nothing about the Empire's purpose, its benefits or its reason for being there at all! Nothing, too, concerning its opponents. **C** gives only a limited range of information compared to **A** or **B**. As such, **C** may be regarded as the least useful evidence of the importance of the British Empire. (8)

Answers to Essay Questions

A. Medieval Realms: Britain 1066–1485

War and Rebellion

1. (a) Describe the main events of the Battle of Hastings. (20)

    ● The Battle of Hastings was fought on 14th October 1066. Harold took up his position on Senlac Hill and his men formed a shieldwall.

    ● In the valley, William arranged his army in three sections: Bretons on the left, Normans in the centre and the Flemish with others on the right.

    ● To the front of each section were archers, then foot soldiers, then knights.

    ● The battle began about 9.30 a.m. when the Norman archers fired on the Saxon shieldwall.

    ● Heavy hand-to-hand fighting then took place against the housecarls with their two-handed axes.

    ● The Norman knights made several attempts to break the Saxon battle line, but failed.

    ● Then the Bretons retreated. It is said that the Normans had tricked the Saxons by pretending to run away. Many Saxon warriors rushed down the hill only to be slaughtered by the Norman knights.

    ● A rumour arose that Duke William had been killed, so to encourage his men, he pushed back his helmet and shouted that he was still alive.

    ● The English lost many men including Gyrth and Leofwine, Harold's brothers. However, as the shieldwall on top of the hill still held fast, William ordered his archers to fire their arrows onto the English.

    ● Harold was wounded with an arrow and then cut down by a Norman knight.

    ● English resistance collapsed and the Saxons were chased from the battlefield.

    ● Most of England's leading men were killed.

    (b) Explain how William I gained control over his new kingdom. (10)

    ● William used castles. At first these were wooden motte-and-bailey types, but later stone keeps appeared, as at Rochester and the Tower of London.

    ● The feudal system was tightened. William gave land to his tenants-in-chief, who in turn controlled the knights, who in turn controlled the peasants.

    ● William crushed rebellions such as that in the North of England (1069) and Hereward the Wake in East Anglia after 1071. He also extended the power of his law courts.

    ● William strengthened his grip on the Church by appointing Norman bishops and Lanfranc as Archbishop of Canterbury.

- The Domesday Book appeared in 1086. This survey of the kingdom, possibly for taxation, gave William I great power.

2. (a) Describe the key details of the civil war between Stephen and Matilda. (20)

- On the death of Henry I in 1135, Stephen of Blois, Henry's nephew seized the Crown in place of Matilda, Henry's daughter.

- Matilda wanted the Crown, so, in 1139, she raised an army to fight Stephen. Civil war followed between the supporters of Stephen and those of Matilda.

- Matilda failed to get support for her cause from the Pope, Innocent II.

- Matilda marched on London to be crowned, but she lost the approval of the city, partly owing to her arrogant and overbearing attitude.

- Stephen was captured at Lincoln in 1141, but Matilda had to free him in return for one of her own men. In 1142, Stephen besieged Oxford and Matilda was forced to flee to Wallingford, escaping from the city across the ice.

- Indecisive warfare continued until 1148 when Matilda returned to Normandy. However, her son, Henry, continued the struggle.

- It was agreed eventually that Henry would take over the Crown when Stephen died.

(b) Explain the main causes of this civil war. (10)

- Henry I's son, William, had been drowned in the *White Ship* disaster in 1120. Matilda, Henry's daughter, was declared heir to the kingdom in the absence of a male candidate.

- The idea of a woman ruler was unpopular with many of the barons and a large group gave their support to Stephen.

- Stephen took the throne as a rival to Matilda, thus making war seem certain.

- Some of the barons did not like Matilda's husband, Geoffrey of Anjou, and so supported Stephen.

- Civil war began when Matilda landed in England in 1139 to stand up for her rights and to claim the English throne.

- The war continued because the nobility were divided between Matilda and Stephen. Many of them also wanted to use the chaos of the war to extend their own wealth and power.

3. (a) Describe the main events of Edward I's campaigns against the Welsh. (20)

- Edward I had a dream of uniting all parts of Britain with himself as overlord.

- In Wales, a prince called Llewelyn had begun to rebel against English rule. Edward I would not allow this, seeing it as a major challenge to his kingly authority.

- Despite several requests, Llewelyn refused homage to Edward in 1274.

- Thus, in 1276–1277, Edward invaded Wales with three armies. He planned his campaign carefully and soon, short of food and supplies, Llewelyn and his supporters were forced to surrender.

- Edward made Llewelyn recognise him as his feudal overlord. Llewelyn resented this, especially as he lost some of his lands.

- In 1282, David, Llewelyn's brother, raised an army, rebelled against the harsh treatment of his fellow countrymen and defeated the English taking seven of their castles.

- Edward I invaded Wales with another army in 1282. He seized Anglesey. Llewelyn was killed in a skirmish at Orewin Bridge.

- Welsh resistance soon collapsed and David was handed over to Edward and brutally executed as a traitor.

(b) Explain what Edward I did to keep control of the Welsh. (10)

- Edward I kept the Welsh under control by building large castles as at Beaumaris, Harlech and Caernarvon. These strongholds provided bases for garrisons of English soldiers who would be on hand to deal with any revolt.

- At Rhuddlan, in 1284, Edward issued the Statute of Wales which imposed a system of order and justice.

- The Welsh were forced to accept English law and administration.

- Welsh lands were divided into counties under English officers.

- New towns were created and these were settled with English people.

- All these factors allowed Edward I to control the Welsh. Welsh independence was finished.

4. (a) Describe the main events of the Battle of Bannockburn. (20)

- Robert Bruce was challenging English authority in Scotland and, in 1314, he threatened Stirling Castle.

- Edward II responded by gathering an army of about 20,000 men. The English and the Scots met at Bannockburn, near Stirling Castle, on 24th June 1314.

- The English army consisted of mounted knights, Welsh archers and foot soldiers.

- The Scots had only between 6,000 and 10,000 men, with few mounted knights. They were led by Robert I.

- The battlefield was surrounded by marshy ground making it impossible for the English knights to outflank the Scots. The Scots were well placed on a wooded ridge above a stream called the Bannock Burn.

- The English attacked the Scots leaving their archers in the rear where they were largely ineffective. The mounted knights failed to break the blocks of Scottish infantry known as schiltrons.

- The Welsh archers were overcome by the Scottish knights. The battle continued and the English were unable to break through the Scottish formations.

- Mistaking large numbers of camp-followers, joining the Scottish ranks, for reinforcements, the English panicked and fled in disorder.

- Many were slaughtered as the Scots swooped down from the ridge. Others drowned in the marshes.

- Edward II narrowly avoided capture. Bannockburn was a great Scottish victory.

(b) Explain how the result of this battle affected Edward II's position as king. (10)

- Defeat at Bannockburn weakened Edward II and he was unable to control powerful barons such as Thomas of Lancaster.

- Respect for the English monarchy under Edward was further weakened.

- Edward II was discredited both at home and in France and was forced to turn again to favourites such as the Dispensers to try to maintain his position as king.

- There were further baronial rebellions and unrest and, although Thomas of Lancaster was defeated and Edward passed the Statute of York, he was eventually overthrown by Isabella and Mortimer in 1327. This demonstrates how fragile his rule was.

- Failure at Bannockburn highlighted Edward's weaknesses as a king, making his barons more determined than ever to seize power and wealth for themselves.

5. (a) Describe the main features of the Battle of Crécy. (20)

- Edward III gathered an army of 12,000 men and landed in Normandy.

- After a long march, Edward arrived at Crécy. He positioned his army on a ridge just outside the village on 26th August 1346. The French had twice as many men as the English.

- In the evening, Philip VI attacked. Rain had wetted the bow-strings of his slow-firing Genoese crossbowmen. They also found themselves shooting into the setting sun.

- From the higher ground, with stakes to the front to defend themselves, the English longbowmen poured arrows onto the Genoese at the rate of up to six a minute.

- The Genoese retreated only to be trampled down by the advancing French knights.

- The English archers fired volley after volley, cutting down the French knights, many of whom were crushed to death or suffocated in their armour.

- The French dead and dying hampered the progress of the following waves of knights. Despite heavy losses, some French knights reached the English line.

- Edward heard that his son, the Black Prince, needed help. It is said that he refused, saying that he should be left alone to earn his spurs.

- The French maintained their attacks fifteen or more times until night fell.

- A wounded Philip VI was led from the battlefield. John, the blind king of Bohemia, fighting as a French ally, was killed.

- Crécy was a glorious English victory. The French lost over 10,000 men and 1,500 lords and knights.

(b) Explain the effects of this battle on the development of the war against France up to 1360. (10)

- Victory at Crécy did not mean the end of the campaign as Edward III was still not king of France, but it gave the English a springboard from which to make further gains.

- Edward, the Black Prince, won a great victory at Poitiers (1356), where John II, the new king of France, was captured.

- This led to the Treaty of Brétigny (1360) by which large areas of France, such as Calais and the territories around Bordeaux, were delivered into English hands.

- Success at Crécy enabled the war to 1360 to be successful for England.

6. (a) Describe the main stages of the Battle of Agincourt. (20)

- In 1415, marching towards Calais, Henry V found his way was blocked by the French under Charles VI.

- The armies met at Agincourt on 25th October. The English were outnumbered having about 7,000 archers and fewer than 1,000 men-at-arms. The French force consisted of around 12,000 men. Estimates vary.

- The English arranged themselves into three blocks of men-at-arms and knights, with archers between them.

- After hours of waiting, Henry ordered his men forward to within 300 yards of the enemy.

- The archers fired bringing down many French knights as their horses were killed.

- Dismounted French knights then dented the English centre, but they were inconvenienced by their heavy armour.

- Henry commanded his archers to drop their bows and to fight the struggling French with swords and daggers. Many knights were killed. Others drowned in the mud.

- A second French attack failed, several noblemen being captured and held to ransom in the chaos and confusion.

- On hearing that the rear of his army was being attacked, Henry ordered the slaughter of many French captives. However, stunned at what was happening, the remaining French fled the battlefield.

- French losses amounted to about 10,000 men. English casualties were around 300.

- Agincourt was an unexpected victory for Henry V and brought him great glory.

(b) Explain why Henry V was able to be victorious in the battle. (10)

- Henry possessed brave, well-disciplined men with high morale. His longbowmen were efficient and the bow was an excellent weapon.

- Henry had a good defensive strategy.

- The mud hampered the heavily-armoured French, but favoured the lightly-clothed English archers.

- The battle site assisted Henry, with woods on either side forcing the French to bunch together as they attacked the English.

- Henry was an inspirational commander. He rallied his men before the conflict. He had also warned his archers that the French planned to cut off the bowstring fingers of any who were captured. This may have frightened them into fighting harder.

- The French charges were ill-disciplined and badly co-ordinated.

- The French commanders squabbled and there was little unity of purpose.

7.　(a) Describe the part played by Joan of Arc in the war against Henry VI.　　(20)

- The English and the Burgundians were gaining power in France. In 1428, they besieged Orléans.

- In France, a peasant girl named Joan, believed that heavenly voices had spoken to her saying that it was her mission to save France from the English.

- Charles VII sent her with the army marching to relieve Orléans.

- Joan inspired the French. She made them believe that God was on their side. This increased their morale, giving them fresh heart for their cause.

- With Joan's encouragement, the French drove the English from Orléans in 1429.

- Joan urged the capture of other English strongholds. She always led her men bravely setting a fine example for them to follow.

- Joan convinced Charles VII to march on Rheims. Charles VII won the city and was crowned king of France. This strengthened the French.

- Joan had reversed the fortunes of war, making the French victorious. She had achieved a military miracle.

- After the failure of the French to capture Paris, Joan began to lose some of her reputation.

- She was captured in 1430 by a Burgundian soldier, handed over to the English and burnt as a witch in Rouen (1431).

- The significance of her role is underlined by the cruelty shown to her by the English before her death.

　(b) Explain how the events of the war against France affected Henry VI's position as king of England.　　(10)

- Henry's position as king had never been strong. As a young boy, effective power lay with his uncles.

- French success weakened his position. Gradually, the French recaptured cities and castles. In 1435, the Duke of Burgundy supported France and, by 1453, the English had lost everything except Calais. This reflected badly on Henry VI.

- Cade's rebellion (1450), caused partly by the loss of Normandy, led to struggles among the nobility. Henry VI became a pawn in a power game.

- English defeats further reduced Henry's fragile influence as barons fought among themselves for political mastery.

- Royal power became ineffective and Henry VI was twice deposed (1461 and 1471). This was in part due to the war.

8. (a) Describe the main details of the Wars of the Roses between 1455 and 1485. (20)

    - A dynastic struggle between the Houses of York and Lancaster developed after Henry VI's mental collapse.

    - In 1459, Margaret of Anjou declared Richard of York a traitor. The Yorkists attacked Calais and Dublin. They seized London, capturing Henry VI.

    - York then made an Act of Accord, leaving Henry VI king but establishing himself as Henry's heir.

    - Margaret raised troops and killed York at Wakefield in 1460. In 1461, at St Albans, the Lancastrians defeated Neville, Earl of Warwick and recaptured Henry VI. Edward, the son of Richard of York, claimed the Crown, joined Warwick and entered London.

    - Edward, now Edward IV, gained victory at Towton (1461). Margaret and Henry VI escaped to Scotland.

    - In 1464, Edward married Elizabeth Woodville bringing many of her supporters to Court. Fearing a loss of political influence, Warwick joined Edward's brother, Clarence, and invaded England. After initial success, Warwick was driven back to France.

    - In 1470, Warwick, with Henry VI and Margaret, again invaded England forcing Edward IV to flee abroad. On his return, he destroyed the Lancastrians at Barnet (killing Warwick) and Tewkesbury, where Henry VI's son died. Henry VI died in the Tower. Edward IV was secure.

    - Edward IV died in 1483 leaving a young heir. Politics were turbulent. Richard of Gloucester took the Crown as Richard III, securing his nephews, Edward and Richard, in the Tower where they disappeared.

    - Richard was defeated and killed at Bosworth (1485), by Henry Tudor, Earl of Richmond, who took the throne as Henry VII.

    (b) Explain the causes of this conflict. (10)

    - Weak monarchy under Henry VI led to a decline in respect for the Crown.

    - The existence of two strong, ambitious, rival aristocratic factions made civil war seem likely.

    - Margaret of Anjou was ambitious for power and control within the kingdom. So were men such as Richard of York, Warwick, Edward IV and the Beauforts.

    - The feudal system had broken down as the nobility became powerful with their private armies.

    - Both central and local government were weak, often overshadowed by aristocratic rivalries.

    - Mismanagement and defeat in the Hundred Years' War also contributed to the conflict.

Government and Parliament

1. (a) Describe the means by which medieval kings between 1066 and 1215 tried to extend control over their realms. (20)

    - Kings used the feudal system. In return for support, they gave land to tenants-in-chief, their most powerful barons and churchmen.

    - Tenants-in-chief paid homage, swearing oaths of fealty as vassals. This provided a mechanism for political, social, economic and military control of the nobility.

    - Kings, despite constant quarrels, worked through the Pope and the Church to ensure that the men they wanted at the top were people they favoured. William I appointed Lanfranc, Henry I brought Anselm back to power and Henry II chose Becket.

    - Castles helped royal control. Castle building developed under William I and Henry I. Henry II controlled castles, being quick to destroy any built illegally.

    - Both Henry I and Henry II extended the rule of law. They strengthened royal justice by encouraging travelling assize courts.

    - Kings like William I, William II, Henry I and Henry II acted quickly to crush rebellions.

    - The production of male heirs to ensure the succession was a vital element of royal authority. William I, Henry II and John were successful in this. Henry I was not.

    - Control was extended abroad. William I was busy in Normandy. Henry II acquired a vast French Empire through his marriage to Eleanor of Aquitaine. Effective kingship meant being constantly active. Henry II spent much time managing his French territories.

    (b) Explain the main factors which determined the success or failure of their various attempts. (10)

    - Kings' personality and character were vital. Strong men like William I and Henry II were successful. Weaker monarchs such as Stephen failed to maintain control.

    - Kings had to pay constant attention to their feudal rights. Rulers like Richard I, who spent only six months of his reign in England, stored up problems for their successors.

    - Success bred strength. Failure led to weakness. John struggled in foreign policy with the loss of Normandy and with the Papacy through the Interdict, generating opposition to his rule.

    - Gender was an issue. Men could succeed, whereas Matilda had problems partly because it was believed women were unfit to have political power.

    - Successful kings to 1215 kept tight control over Normandy and the rest of their French Empire.

2. (a) Describe the main elements of the baronial revolts against King John. (20)

- The barons were upset with John's failures in foreign policy including the loss of Normandy (1204).

- They hated John for his lack of success with Innocent III resulting in the placing of England under Interdict and the surrender of the country as a Papal Fief.

- The barons objected to John's abuse of unwritten feudal customs. He had overcharged for reliefs, taken scutage when there was no war, raised high taxes himself and allowed unfair treatment in the law courts.

- John's refusal to meet his barons led them to raise an army and force him to sign Magna Carta at Runnymede in June 1215.

- Through Magna Carta, the barons had restricted royal power to their advantage.

- The Charter stated that John was to leave the Church alone; he was forbidden to raise taxes without baronial approval; baronial control was exercised over reliefs and scutage; freemen could not be imprisoned or punished without a fair trial. John was not to sell or deny justice to anyone.

(b) Explain the importance of Magna Carta. (10)

- Magna Carta demonstrated that monarchs could be controlled by the action of a powerful baronage.

- It showed that the barons were keen to protect themselves against any encroachment on their powers.

- John was ordered to rule according to the customs of the kingdom and a committee of 25 barons was to keep a check on him.

- The presentation of the Charter, although a response to immediate problems, set a pattern for further similar baronial action.

- The Charter laid down the standards to be observed by future kings and it provided the first written definition of royal rights.

- Basic rights and liberties concerning justice, taxation and freedom had been aired and recorded and would filter down to ordinary people in the course of time.

- Such was its importance that some of its chapters remain on the Statute Book and the essence of Magna Carta underpins the law of the land to this very day.

3. (a) Describe the main events of the Peasants' Revolt. (20)

- In 1381, the revolt began with Poll Tax riots in Brentwood, Essex. Throughout May and June, peasant uprisings spread, especially in Essex and Kent. Many tradesmen, priests and friars joined in.

- Legal officials and tax collectors were attacked.

- John Ball, the 'mad' priest, and Wat Tyler inflamed the rebels leading them to London to seek reforms from Richard II.

- Rioting occurred in London. John of Gaunt's Savoy Palace was burnt, as were the Inns of Court. Foreigners were beaten up.

- Richard II left the Tower, rode to Mile End, met the rebels and agreed to their demands concerning higher wages and the abolition of villeinage.

- Some rebels returned home. Others burst into the Tower, seized Simon Sudbury (Chancellor and Archbishop of Canterbury) and Robert Hales (Lord Treasurer), and beheaded them on Tower Hill.

- Richard II met the rebels on 15th June at Smithfield. Tyler made more demands: lordships (except that of the king) were to be abolished and Church lands were to be given to the people. Richard agreed.

- A scuffle occurred. Tyler was wounded by the Mayor of London and killed by a royal attendant. Richard then shouted to the peasants, that he would be their captain. Some rebels left immediately. The rest dispersed when armed men appeared from London.

- Richard's promises were not kept. Rebel leaders, like John Ball, were hunted down and hanged.

(b) Explain why the revolt occurred. (10)

- The Black Death (1348–1350) led to a shortage of labour. Peasants demanded higher wages and better conditions.

- The Statute of Labourers (1351) was passed to keep wages down.

- Feudal conditions varied. Some lords allowed their villeins to exchange labour services for money rents. Others did not. On Church lands, some abbots and bishops strictly enforced all labour services.

- Peasants resented their lords' privileges and power.

- The war with France was going badly. This contributed to the social tensions of the late 1370s.

- The whole power of the Church over the people was questioned.

- The trigger causes of the revolt were the Poll Taxes of 1377, 1379 and 1381.

4. (a) Describe the main features of the Model Parliament of 1295. (20)

- The Model Parliament was summoned by Edward I in November 1295 to grant money for his wars.

- It was called 'model' by William Stubbs, a 19th-century historian who thought it was the most representative Parliament ever called up to that date, and that it formed an exact model for future Parliaments.

- It was attended by lords, bishops and archbishops, abbots, delegates for the lesser clergy, two knights from each shire, representing the countryside, and burgesses from the towns.

- These were organised into two houses: the Lords (barons and bishops), and the Commons with the knights and burgesses.

- There were no political parties and no representatives of the peasants or lesser folk.

- The number of men who attended was over 400.

- The assembly of King, lords and commons represented the idea of a community of the realm, when the monarch could meet his more important subjects for help in ruling the country.

- The Parliament passed statutes (laws) and these became the highest form of authority in the kingdom.

- Sometimes the Commons made petitions (requests) to Edward. If he agreed with them, these requests became law.

(b) Explain how far this event was important in the development of Parliament. (10)

- The Model Parliament was an impressive assembly. It was important to the future development of Parliament, but this importance has been exaggerated.

- Earlier parliamentary writs (commands to attend Parliament) show that assemblies before 1295 were also composed of king, lords, burgesses and knights of the shire.

- Neither did the Model Parliament set the precise pattern for future Parliaments as the lesser clergy ceased to be summoned.

- Nonetheless, it did help to develop the general idea of government by King, lords and commons, with the indirect representation of many of the king's subjects.

- It also helped the growth of Statute Law which became the basis of law for the judges to interpret.

- The Model Parliament with its variety of business also helped to shape the function of future Parliaments, a major one being the granting of money to the king.

5. (a) Describe the struggles between Henry II and Thomas Becket. (20)

- In 1162, Henry II appointed his friend, Thomas Becket, as Archbishop of Canterbury. Henry believed this would enable him to increase his control over the Church.

- Becket said that his duty to the Church must come before his duty to the king.

- Henry and Becket quarrelled over the issue of criminous clerks. Churchmen who had done wrong were tried and punished in Church courts. Henry wanted churchmen sentenced in his own courts, so that he could increase his power and receive money from fines.

- In 1164, through the Constitutions of Clarendon, Henry tried to impose his will. Becket opposed the king's wishes and went into exile in France.

- Underlying the legal struggle, was the question of who was really in charge in England – Henry or the Church.

- Becket returned to England in 1170.

- Becket complained to the Pope because, in his absence, the Archbishop of York had crowned Henry's young son. Becket excommunicated all clergy connected with the coronation.

- In France, Henry II was told that Becket had been misusing his power. In a fit of rage, he shouted, 'Who will rid me of this turbulent priest?'

- Four knights, thinking to please the king, took Henry at his word, sailed to England and murdered Becket at Canterbury on 29th December 1170.

(b) Explain the effects of Becket's murder on Henry II. (10)

- Henry's attempts to extend control over the Church failed. In 1172, at Avranches (Normandy), he was forced to end all new customs harmful to the Church.

- Henry regretted his angry words and was saddened by the death of his friend. He did penance by walking in simple robes through the streets of Canterbury while the cathedral monks whipped him.

- Henry's reputation suffered. He was blamed for Becket's death and everyone waited for God to punish him.

- Becket's murder made Henry appear in the wrong, especially when Pope Alexander III made Becket a saint in 1173.

- The Christian world was shocked by Becket's death and Henry had to beg for readmission to the favour of the Church.

Religion

1. (a) Describe the ideal routines of daily life inside a medieval monastery. (20)

- The Rule of St Benedict (c.480–c.543) shaped a monk's routine. This divided the day into three periods: prayer, study and manual labour. Benedict believed that 'Idleness is the enemy of the soul', so monks were kept busy.

- At 2.00 a.m. a bell summoned the monks to church for Mattins and Lauds.

- Prime was held at 6.00 a.m., followed perhaps by an early Mass. Breakfast of bread and ale came next.

- At about 9.00 a.m., the monks attended Terce. This was followed by a meeting in the chapter house. Here, a chapter from St Benedict's Rule was read and monks were given their daily tasks. Monastery business was discussed. Any wrongdoers received their punishments from the abbot.

- At about 11.00 a.m., a High Mass was held followed by dinner, the main meal of the day. This might consist of soup, bread, meat, eggs, cheese, fruit, honey, wine or water and, on certain days, fish.

- After a short rest, the monks went to church for Nones.

- Then came manual work perhaps in the fields, the workshop, the mill or the bakery. During this time, some monks might study in the cloister or write in the scriptorium.

- Vespers was held at about 6.00 p.m., after which came supper. The final service of Compline took place at about 9.00 p.m. Then to bed and silence until the Mattins' bell rang out the start of the next day's routine.

(b) Explain why monasteries had become so powerful by 1500.   (10)

- Wealthy men and women often gave money and jewels to monasteries hoping that his might help them get to Heaven.

- Monasteries often received grants of land. The extent of monastic power can be measured by the fact that around 1500, they owned about one third of the land in England.

- Monasteries gained power by taking over the right to appoint vicars to parish churches. This meant monks could take some of the taxes paid to priests.

- Monasteries, like Winchester, owned several manors and drew power from the income from their farming.

- Others, such as Canterbury and Durham, received money from pilgrims visiting the shrines of their saints.

2.   (a) Describe the events of the church career of John Wycliffe.   (20)

- Born in Yorkshire and educated at Oxford, Wycliffe was a religious reformer and a leading 14th-century thinker.

- He denounced clerical wealth and privilege, arguing that because the Church was unholy, it should lose its property. When condemned by the Pope in 1377, he was protected by his patron, John of Gaunt and by Oxford University.

- After 1378, he widened his attacks on clerical subjects such as Papal authority, confession, monasteries and transubstantiation (the Catholic belief that the consecrated bread is transformed into the actual body of Christ).

- In 1381, many in the Peasants' Revolt took up Wycliffe's ideas, although he was not directly associated with the rebellion.

- Wycliffe's passionate belief in the authority of God's Word as a means of attaining Grace, led him to begin his own translation of the Bible.

- However, his criticism of the Mass went too far, and he was condemned both by Oxford University (1381–1382) and Courtenay, the Archbishop of Canterbury, being forced to retire to his parish at Lutterworth.

(b) Explain why he is seen as such an important figure of the medieval Church.   (10)

- Wycliffe is seen as important because he founded the Lollard movement in England and made people more aware of the Church's faults.

- Some believe that Wycliffe's criticisms of the Church look forward, via John Hus in Bohemia, to the Lutheran and Protestant Reformation of the 16th century.

- Many of his ideas about preaching in English and making an English translation of the Bible were achieved at the Reformation.

- Wycliffe challenged the Church's authority and forced it to defend itself and its practices.

- On the other hand, many of Wycliffe's followers were artisans and farmers with negative and simplistic ideas.

- The Lollard Bible – a literal and almost unreadable translation from the Latin – damaged the case for making an authorised translation into English.

- Wycliffe himself did nothing to inspire the Reformation and it may be argued that his followers discredited even moderate reform.

- Nonetheless, Wycliffe remains an important figure not only for his ideas, but because there is so much controversy about him and his achievements.

3. (a) Describe the main events of the Third Crusade. (20)

- In 1187, under Saladin, the Muslims recaptured much of the Holy Land. Jerusalem and many other Christian cities fell.

- The Pope called for a crusade to save Palestine. Richard I, Phillip II of France and Emperor Frederick I of Germany took up the cross.

- Richard travelled by sea via Cyprus, which he captured. He married Berengaria of Navarre. Philip arrived safely in the Holy Land. Frederick drowned on the way and most of his army went home.

- Richard came to Acre. Despite illness, he directed the siege and captured the city in July 1191.

- A truce was made with Saladin. Philip II returned to France. Richard was now in command.

- In August 1191, Richard marched on Jaffa. He beat off a Muslim attack at Arsuf and captured Jaffa.

- Richard then moved inland and camped 12 miles from Jerusalem. He was short of men and supplies. He came within sight of the walls, but it is said that he shielded his eyes, refusing to look at what he was unable to take.

- An agreement was made with Saladin, who promised that the crusaders could keep all conquered towns down to Jaffa and that Christians could visit the Holy Places in peace.

- In return, the Crusaders had to surrender all their strongholds south of Jaffa.

(b) Explain whether or not you believe this crusade was a success. (10)

- The Crusade failed in the sense that Jerusalem had not been recaptured and that Saladin remained supreme there and in the surrounding area.

- However, there were some successful aspects.

- It showed the Pope's power in being able to encourage European rulers to take up arms in the cause of the Church.

- The Christian presence in parts of the Holy Land was strengthened and Saladin's influence had been challenged.

- Trade with the East was stimulated and luxury items were increasingly imported into Europe.

- Maritime business in the Mediterranean was extended and developments in shipping, navigation and even naval warfare were stimulated.

- Cultural contacts with the Middle East were increased.

4. (a) Describe the usual duties of a hard-working village priest in medieval England. (20)

- A good village priest stayed in his parish looking after his flock and carrying out a range of duties.

- He took services in the Church. The most important was Mass, held every Sunday and on Holy Days. This was in Latin, but a priest should say a few words in English. He might preach about the Ten Commandments, teach a few simple prayers or Bible stories such as Adam and Eve or Noah's Ark.

- If a church had wall-paintings like The Last Judgement, showing devils tormenting the damned while saved souls were carried to Heaven by angels, the priest used this to explain that unless people believed and followed their religion, they would go to Hell.

- He should also tell the villagers about Heaven, as a paradise they could attain by being good Christians.

- An industrious priest also baptised babies, married couples and buried the dead.

- Hard-working priests educated bright village boys, teaching them how to read and write, passing on perhaps a few words of Latin.

- They visited the sick and dying, and gave alms and food to the poor.

- A caring priest maintained the fabric of his church and his house.

- A diligent man also cultivated his glebe (his land) and collected his tithes from the villagers. At busy times, such as at harvest, he worked in the fields.

(b) Explain why a good priest was so important to a village community during the Middle Ages. (10)

- It was important for the villagers to have a good example set before them. If the priest were evil, how could they be good?

- Villagers needed someone to look after their spiritual life and to offer a way to Heaven through the forgiving of sins.

- A hard-working priest was necessary to encourage people to lead a Christian life, following basic rules like the Ten Commandments.

- He was also a person to whom villagers could turn to discuss their troubles and problems.

- A conscientious priest would also assist with order and discipline within a village, helping to resolve personal disputes.

Social History

1. (a) Describe the main details of the development of the Black Death in England
       from 1348 to 1349.   (20)

   - In June 1348, the Black Death arrived in Melcombe (Dorset). It had spread to
     England from Asia via the Middle East. It was brought by European trading ships.

   - The disease was carried by fleas living on black rats. A person became infected by
     suffering a flea-bite.

   - Symptoms included the appearance of large buboes, vomiting, the formation of black
     blotches over the body, intense pain and, usually, death after about three to five days.

   - Medical knowledge was limited. The causes of the illness were not understood, still
     less its treatment. Remedies like purifying the air with smoke and herbs proved
     ineffectual.

   - Lucky victims survived if their buboes burst, releasing a foul-smelling puss.

   - The plague was widespread in ports such as Bristol and Southampton. It struck
     towns like Gloucester, Norwich and Oxford. In London, 43% of its 70,000
     inhabitants died.

   - In the countryside, villages suffered likewise as the disease covered most of England
     by December 1348.

   - Many churchmen died as priests tried to minister to the victims. The death-rate
     among Herefordshire clergy reached nearly 47%.

   - So many people died so quickly that their bodies were dumped into huge plague
     pits. England's population was reduced by around one third.

   (b) Explain the effects of the Black Death on life in the countryside.   (10)

   - The Black Death had considerable effects on life in the countryside.

   - Whole villages were wiped out. These are now known as 'Deserted Medieval
     Villages'.

   - Empty cottages fell into ruin and grass grew over the paths and track ways.

   - Unploughed fields became overgrown. Animals were left unattended.

   - Food prices rose as crop production fell.

   - In some places, innocent women were accused of being witches who had started
     the epidemic. Some were killed by mobs.

   - Universal misery was the hallmark of rural life.

   - One long-term effect was a shortage of peasant labour which encouraged many to
     leave their village in search of better wages and conditions. Parliament took action
     to keep wages to pre-plague levels through the Statute of Labourers (1351). This led
     to peasant unrest, which in turn helped to cause the Peasants' Revolt of 1381.

2. (a) Describe the key features of peasant life in a medieval village. (20)

- A villein's home consisted of a two-roomed timber-framed thatched cottage with a patch of garden for vegetables. The earthen floor was strewn with rushes. An open fire burnt on a stone slab. A hole in the roof let out the smoke. Wooden shutters protected the small windows.

- The cottages were dark and smelly as chickens, dogs and even pigs shared the living space.

- Food comprised pottage, eggs, milk, cheese, fruit, vegetables, bread, weak beer, occasional fish and very occasional meat.

- Apart from attending Church, peasants spent most of their time working, labouring on both the lord's land and their own strips in the open fields. In the autumn, the main tasks consisted of ploughing, killing livestock and salting the meat for winter food.

- During winter, peasants cleared ditches, repaired hedges, buildings and tools, kept warm and tried to survive.

- Spring saw more ploughing, hoeing and weeding. Animals were grazed on the fallow field.

- Summer was the busiest time, first with cutting hay, then the corn harvest when the whole village laboured to bring in the crops. After this, women gleaned over the stubble. The next tasks were threshing and winnowing the corn.

- Sundays were rest days. There were entertainments on Saints' Days. At May Time, peasants danced around the maypole. There was often a Christmas feast in the lord's hall.

(b) Explain how a lord of the manor ran his village. (10)

- Lords ran their villages through the feudal system which gave them social and economic control. Peasants were allotted land in return for labour services. These were listed in documents known as Extents, so lords could exact full services.

- The reeve (the lord's agent) or bailiff ensured that all work was done.

- The Manor Court provided legal control. The lord punished offenders and ensured that all manorial customs were kept.

- Peasants were not allowed to leave the manor, or marry, without the lord's permission. On a villein's death, a son could not take over his father's land without authorisation and the payment of a fine.

- Through the feudal system a peasant's land, his home, even his very person, were the lord's property.

General Topics

1. (a) Describe the part played by women in medieval life. (20)

  - Social status largely determined the part played by women.

  - Queens, such as Matilda and Eleanor of Aquitaine, took an important role in politics, even though it was thought that women should not engage in such activities.

  - Aristocratic ladies directed their household's economy and managed their servants. They were often parties to arranged marriages made to secure family fortunes.

  - Upper-class widows were sometimes granted land and achieved limited independence after the death of their husbands.

  - Gentlewomen might have to defend their manor houses, as did Margaret Paston in 15th-century Norfolk.

  - Gentry ladies went into nunneries where life was often easy and they could rise to positions of influence like Chaucer's Prioress in *The Canterbury Tales*.

  - In towns, merchants' wives looked after their houses and families. They might help their husband with his trade, or even go to market themselves selling items like eggs, butter and cheese.

  - Many women baked bread or brewed ale.

  - Peasant women were kept busy. Their tasks included raising a family, managing the household, looking after their men, working in the fields at harvest time and gleaning after the corn had been gathered. They also spun wool, fetched water and carried corn to the mill.

  - A few individuals, like Joan of Arc, gained fame, but most women's lives were shaped by their marriage, home and family. Few had the chance to stand alone.

 (b) Explain why women were not seen as being equal to men in medieval times. (10)

  - The prevailing medieval view was that women were the weaker vessel and therefore inferior to men.

  - The Church saw women's secondary rank as part of a God-given order of things.

  - Eve, being created from one of Adam's ribs, was seen as second class. Thus, the social position of women was defined.

  - Also influential was the New Testament idea that husband and wife were one. This led to the surrender of a woman's possessions to her husband on marriage.

  - It was thought that women were unfit to hold political power or to play any major role in public affairs.

2. (a) Describe the main developments in the style of castle building from 1066 to around 1500. (20)

  - Motte-and-bailey castles flourished after 1066. These were quick and easy to construct.

- A motte (mound) was formed by digging a circular ditch and throwing the earth into the middle. The keep (a wooden tower where the lord lived) was built on the flattened motte.

- The bailey, an enclosed living space surrounded by a dry ditch and a wooden palisade, was linked to the motte by a drawbridge. Often, the bailey entrance also had a drawbridge.

- Later, circular, stone keeps (shell keeps) developed, like Windsor and Tamworth.

- During the 1100s, great, square, stone tower keeps came into fashion, as at Dover and Rochester. These had thick walls and corner towers. Accommodation was arranged over several floors from the dungeons and store rooms in the basement, up through the great hall, dormitories and battlements to wall-walks at the top.

- The main entrance, at the side, was protected by a drawbridge.

- The 1200s featured concentric castles, as at Beaumaris, with rings of curtain walls, one within the other, like concentric circles. Mural towers re-enforced the walls. They usually had a well-defended barbican gatehouse.

- In the later Middle Ages, large castles were no longer built. Warfare centred mainly on battlefields.

- The need for defence remained, but castles became fortified manor houses like Stoksey Castle and Minster Lovell.

(b) Explain why medieval castles were built in particular places. (10)

- After 1066, castles were constructed wherever William I sensed opposition.

- Others occupied ancient sites fortified by the Romans or Saxons at important road junctions.

- Some were erected on natural, defensive sites protected by high cliffs or water. Leeds Castle (Kent) was built on an island.

- Others were built to protect England, as at Carlisle, which guarded the west end of the Scottish border.

- Edward I's castles, like Harlech and Caernarvon, both protected England and controlled the Welsh.

- Other sites defended important river crossings and bridges, as at Rochester and Conway.

- Castles like Dover and Bamburgh guarded ports and the coast.

- Their general purpose was to maintain royal authority in key areas. They had both a defensive and offensive role.

3. (a) Describe the key features of the career of Simon de Montfort. (20)

- Simon de Montfort, Earl of Leicester, married to the king's sister, emerged as leader of the baronial opposition to Henry III from 1258 to 1265.

- Rebellion began owing to baronial jealousy over the king's use of foreigners to run his government. Many of these received estates and Henry allowed the Pope to appoint over 300 foreign clergy to English churches.

- Henry had also ignored Magna Carta.

- Simon helped to draw up the Provisions of Oxford. In a Parliament at Oxford (1258), he led the barons as they pressed their demands on the king. Henry agreed to banish foreigners and to obey the Great Charter.

- Some barons, jealous of Simon's power, encouraged Henry to oppose him. Louis IX of France denounced the Provisions of Oxford.

- Henry and Prince Edward raised an army, but were defeated and captured by Simon at the battle of Lewes (1264). De Montfort was now virtual ruler of England.

- Simon called a Parliament to which came knights and townsmen, as well as lords and churchmen. He hoped to win support but failed.

- Prince Edward had escaped. He gathered an army and Simon was beaten and killed at Evesham (1265). His family lost their estates and their castle at Kenilworth.

(b) Explain why he may be regarded by historians as a failure or a success.   (10)

- Simon's death and defeat at Evesham suggest failure in the short term.

- There were many long-term consequences. Royal authority had been challenged and future kings could not ignore the demands of their nobles.

- Simon's Parliament, with a widespread selection of representatives, formed a blueprint for the future development of Parliament.

- Some medieval writers saw him as a success. Matthew Paris praised Simon's struggle for freedom and justice.

- He was viewed at the time as a martyr for liberty. A cult emerged and Evesham Abbey (housing his remains) became a centre of pilgrimage and miracles.

- Argument rages. Some historians minimise Simon's contribution to the development of Parliament. Others see the baronial reform movement as a formative part of the development of England's constitution and as an important step along the road to democracy.

4.   (a) Describe the main features of the career and work of the poet, Geoffrey Chaucer. (20)

- Chaucer was born around 1340 and died in 1400. The son of a prosperous London vintner, he became a diplomat and poet.

- After serving as an esquire and page in aristocratic households, Chaucer entered royal service in 1357. He fought in the Hundred Years' War. After being captured and ransomed in the 1359 Brittany campaign, he travelled abroad on royal business.

- While visiting Genoa and Florence (1372–1375), he acquired a familiarity with French and Italian poetry styles.

- From 1374 to 1386, he held the well-paid post of Controller of Customs in the Port of London, after which he became MP for Kent. Chaucer was Clerk of the King's Works from 1389 to 1391, receiving a pension from Henry IV in 1399.

- Chaucer's life experiences show through in his poems. He visited elite households and a courtly audience is suggested by much of his writing.

- In many of his works, he used established sources such as Froissart, Dante, Petrarch and Classical authors like Virgil and Ovid.

- Chaucer's best-known work, written about 1384, is *The Canterbury Tales*, a collection of 23 stories by pilgrims as they journeyed to Canterbury.

- Some characters, like the knight and the poor parson, represent an ideal. Others such as the monk and the prioress fall short of their callings. Chaucer pokes gentle fun at them for not behaving as they should.

- Other poems include his tragedy, *Troilus and Criseyde*.

(b) Explain why he should be regarded as an important medieval writer. (10)

- Chaucer is important in using Middle English, rather than Latin in his poems. Thus, he made a notable impact on the development of English literature and language.

- In *The Canterbury Tales*, Chaucer offers valuable details of such people as a knight, squire, merchant, lawyer, miller and several churchmen.

- Their activities are described, so this poem is important as social history.

- His writings are thus important as they reveal contemporary jokes and attitudes. For example, his line about an honest miller having a golden thumb suggests that millers were considered dishonest, as no man could literally have a thumb made of gold.

- Chaucer also provides many details of medieval life, such as pilgrimages.

5. (a) Describe some of the main details of the Bayeux Tapestry. (20)

- The Bayeux Tapestry is about 20 inches wide and 230 feet long. Through a series of 72 pictures, it tells the story of the Norman Conquest of England in 1066. The scenes have Latin comments, making it a sort of strip cartoon.

- In was embroidered by English ladies sometime before 1082 and was probably made for Odo of Bayeux, William's half-brother, who features throughout the action.

- The story begins with Edward the Confessor's death and shows Harold's Brittany campaign, his oath to William, his return to England and coronation by Stigand. It then depicts William's anger, Norman preparations for invasion, the invasion itself, followed by the Battle of Hastings and Harold's death.

- It is incomplete, but a final scene illustrates the English being chased off into the woods, one still clutching an arrow shaft in his eye.

- As a work of art, with the Conqueror as hero, the final section originally may have illustrated William I in triumph on the English throne, but we cannot know this.

- The borders contain scenes from medieval life, such as ploughing and harrowing. At the battle, the lower border is filled with dead and wounded men. Bodies are stripped of their armour. Elsewhere are strange birds and beasts.

- Sometimes the main action is reflected in the margins, as when William brings in his archers.

- The tapestry has a moral message showing the fate of a man (Harold) who has broken an oath.

(b) Explain why it is such an important piece of evidence for historians. (10)

- It is an important pictorial source for the Norman Conquest. Biased to the Normans, it is a piece of Norman propaganda showing us how they viewed events.

- The tapestry is the only detailed primary source suggesting how Harold died.

- Much material is provided concerning weapons, armour, fighting tactics, horses and their use with long stirrups and double bridles.

- Also featured are details of buildings, clothes, as well as the construction and management of ships.

- The actual fabric enables historians to learn about how tapestries were made, the kind of thread used, the styles of stitching and the dyes to make the colouring.

B. The Making of the United Kingdom: 1485–1750

War and Rebellion

1. (a) Describe how Henry VII gained the crown in 1485. (20)

- Henry VII had the chance to pursue the throne owing to the weakening of the monarchy and the breakdown of effective English government in the years after 1455.

- Rival aristocratic factions had exhausted each other, allowing Henry to stake his claim.

- Edward IV and Richard III never attained complete support. Richard III was very popular in the north of England, but the southern nobility were unsure of him.

- In 1483, Richard III did not have the best title to the throne. Doubts over his right to be king and his ruthlessness to his nephews weakened his position.

- Henry Tudor claimed the throne through his mother, Lady Margaret Beaufort, who represented a line going back to John of Gaunt. Although this had been declared illegitimate, Henry made the most of it. After all, his father was half-brother to Henry VI and his grandmother had been Henry V's queen.

- After his son's death (1484) Richard III had no heir to succeed him.

- Richard III was unpopular, so Henry gained support, not least from Charles VIII of France.

- In 1485, Henry took his chance, invaded England and gained the Crown through victory at Bosworth.

- Henry was shrewd. Thus, he dated the start of his reign from the day before Bosworth as if to suggest that his claim to the throne was not just based on one victory.

(b) Explain why he was victorious at the Battle of Bosworth. (10)

- Luck and circumstances, as well as skill, enabled Henry to be victorious at Bosworth.

- Although Richard had more men, he could not trust his commanders, many of whom were suspicious of each other.

- Many Yorkists were not loyal to their king.

- Northumberland's men, in the rear of his battle-line, did little to support Richard.

- The Stanleys with 3,000 men remained neutral at the beginning of the battle, until they attacked Richard's troops, thus handing victory to Henry VII.

2. (a) Describe the main events of the Pilgrimage of Grace. (20)

- In 1536, opposition to the closure of smaller monasteries, rising prices, extension of enclosures, government interference in elections and corruption of officials, led to an uprising against Henry VIII known as the Pilgrimage of Grace.

- The rebellion began in Louth. About 10,000 rebels attacked Lincoln, but were dispersed by the Duke of Norfolk.

- Unrest spread to Cumberland and Westmorland.

- In Yorkshire, about 30,000 rebels, led by Robert Aske, a lawyer, and Lord Darcy, marched on York.

- Their demands included the sacking of heretical churchmen, like Cranmer, the repeal of certain Acts of the Reformation Parliament and the punishment of Thomas Cromwell. Also, they wished to make legitimate Princess Mary's claim to the throne.

- Aske claimed that his followers were pilgrims, not rebels. They marched with religious banners and wore badges symbolising the five wounds of Christ.

- Further demands included the refusal to pay any new taxes and freedom of speech in the House of Commons.

- At Doncaster, Norfolk, acting on the king's instructions, promised that rebel grievances would be heard in a Parliament summoned to York.

- Many rebels thus returned home.

- In January 1537, Henry VIII took bloody revenge on the remainder. Over 200 were executed.

- Aske was hanged in chains at York and, in July, Lord Darcy, who had surrendered Pontefract Castle to the rebels, was beheaded on Tower Hill.

(b) Explain why this rebellion failed. (10)

- The uprising failed owing to the power and strength of the Tudor monarchy.

- Norfolk showed skill in delaying the rebels with promises, while Henry marshalled his forces.

- The authorities were clever in splitting the leaders from the masses and the gentry from the commoners.

- The promise of pardons caused the majority to return home.

- The rebels lacked food or supplies. They had no clear plan and their protest was unco-ordinated.

- Disunity among the rebels weakened their cause. Some wanted religious reform, while others had social and political concerns.

3. (a) Describe the main details of Kett's Rebellion and the Prayer Book Rising of 1549. (20)

- Two uprisings faced Edward VI in 1549. The Prayer Book Rebellion was a protest against the advancement of Protestantism as part of the English Reformation.

- Cranmer had introduced a Protestant Prayer Book, in English, in 1549. Two years earlier, he had abolished chantries.

- In areas of traditional religion, such as Devon and Cornwall, people rebelled against these changes. They believed that the old gateways to Heaven had been closed and that their souls were in danger.

- The rebels demanded a return to former Catholic practices and a delay in further religious changes.

- Exeter was besieged. After a struggle, government troops under Lord Russell regained control. The protestors were scattered. Many were killed.

- Kett's Rebellion, in July 1549, was more a protest against economic hardship.

- In East Anglia, unrest grew owing to enclosures, rising unemployment, high land rents and the loss of common fishing rights.

- Protest camps were established in Ipswich and Bury St Edmunds. Robert Kett and a rebel force seized Norwich.

- Government forces commanded by the Earl of Warwick defeated Kett's followers on Mousehold Heath, where around 3,000 rebels were slaughtered.

- Kett was captured and hanged as a traitor from the walls of Norwich Castle.

(b) Explain why the rebels were unsuccessful. (10)

- The Tudor monarchy was too strong for either of these rebellions to succeed.

- The Tudors feared rebellion from below and always took harsh measures to crush any uprisings. This was especially so in 1549 when these two rebellions posed a serious threat to Edward VI's government.

- Any sympathy that Somerset may have had for the rebels' cause was easily overcome in the Council.

- Edward's commanders were better equipped and organised, so they crushed the uprisings easily.

- The rebels were disunited. They lacked a common purpose and this generated weakness.

- The rebels lacked the necessary supplies and weapons to maintain a successful campaign.

- Neither protest was significant enough to attract the level of support necessary for national success.

4. (a) Describe the important features of the Lady Jane Grey plot. (20)

- Throughout 1552, Edward VI's health grew worse. He died on 6th July 1553. By the terms of Henry VIII's will, the throne was now Mary's, but the Duke of Northumberland planned to exclude Catholic Mary in favour of a Protestant.

- Northumberland persuaded Edward to leave the throne to the children of Lady Jane Grey, great granddaughter of Henry VIII's sister, Mary.

- To ensure there were children, Northumberland bullied Jane into marrying his fourth son, Lord Guilford Dudley. His aim was to enjoy real power over his son and daughter-in-law.

- When it became obvious that Edward would die before Jane had children, the will was altered to give the throne to Jane herself.

- Upon Edward's death, Jane Grey was proclaimed queen at the Tower, where she promised to look after the religion and laws of her kingdom.

- Mary escaped to Norfolk and Suffolk, strong Catholic areas. She wrote to the Council demanding that they recognise her rights as queen.

- Mary gathered troops at Framlingham Castle. Support for Northumberland dwindled. More and more of the Council supported Mary. On 19th July, Mary was declared queen in London.

- Northumberland surrendered without a fight, hoping for mercy. He was executed in August 1553.

- In the Tower, Jane Grey exchanged her state rooms for a dungeon. Her reign had lasted nine days.

- Mary arrived in London to a triumphal welcome.

- Jane Grey and her husband went to the block early in 1554.

(b) Explain the main effects of this plot on the monarchy. (10)

- The plot ensured the legitimate succession of Mary Tudor.

- It ended speculation about the succession after the uncertainty caused by Northumberland's plotting.

- It helped to make sure that proper arrangements were in place for the succession of immediate future monarchs.

- The plot raised people's awareness of succession problems and, from then on, the claims of pretenders received only modest support.

- It brought in a popular monarch who became hated owing to her Catholicism, thus it indirectly ensured the ultimate triumph of Protestantism under the English monarchy.

5. (a) Describe the career of Mary Queen of Scots after her arrival in England. (20)

- In May 1568, after defeat at the Battle of Langside, Catholic Mary, Queen of Scots abdicated her throne and fled to England seeking refuge with her cousin Elizabeth I.

- Mary was held as a virtual prisoner for 19 years, moving from manor house to manor house and estate to estate until the discovery of the Babington Plot sealed her fate.

- In 1569, Mary was associated with the Northern Rebellion. Elizabeth had discovered plans for Mary's marriage to the Duke of Norfolk. Norfolk was sent to the Tower causing a revolt by his supporters led by the Earls of Northumberland and Westmorland. The uprising was crushed. Security around Mary was tightened.

- The failure of the Ridolfi Plot (1571), a scheme to free Mary and promote the Catholic cause, again caused increased suspicion of Mary.

- Mary was implicated in the Throckmorton Plot (1583) and the Babington Plot (1586), each of which had as its aim Mary's liberation and her accession to the English throne.

- Burghley, Elizabeth's chief minister, working through Francis Walsingham, was determined to prove Mary guilty of treason, thereby ensuring her execution. It is impossible to say just how far Mary was involved in these plots. Some evidence may have been forged by Burghley's agents.

- Failure of the plots brought Mary to trial for treason in 1586. She was found guilty. Although Elizabeth delayed signing the death warrant, Mary was executed at Fotheringhay Castle in February 1587.

(b) Explain the ways in which Mary was dangerous to Elizabeth I. (10)

- Mary was a danger to Elizabeth owing to her position in the dynastic struggles between England, France and Scotland.

- As a Roman Catholic in a Protestant country, Mary posed a religious threat.

- Mary was a risk as she became the centre of Roman Catholic plots which threatened Elizabeth's control over her kingdom.

- Mary was dangerous politically. She had a good claim to the throne as heir to Elizabeth, whom many Catholics did not regard as the true successor to the English crown.

- While Elizabeth was unmarried, the possibility remained that Mary might come to the English throne.

6. (a) Describe the main events of the war with Spain 1588–1603. (20)

- In 1588, England and Spain went to war. Politically, England supported the Protestant Dutch against Catholic Spain. Spain helped Irish rebels against England. Philip II was determined to reconvert England to Roman Catholicism. There was rivalry in the New World and Africa over slaves and gold.

- The execution of Mary, Queen of Scots, and Drake's raid on Cadiz in 1587, were trigger causes of the war.

- Philip II sent a fleet of about 130 ships against England. The aim was to defeat the English navy in the Channel, winning command of the sea, link up with Parma's army in the Spanish Netherlands and invade England.

- The Armada was sighted off the Lizard in July 1588. A running battle followed, with skirmishes off Plymouth, Portland Bill and the Isle of Wight. The Spanish took refuge in Calais harbour.

- The English sent in fire ships. This marked the end of the Armada as a disciplined fighting force. They fled northwards pursued by the English. Many ships were wrecked on the Scottish and Irish coasts. Only around 86 ships returned to Spain.

- The direct threat was over, but war continued. In 1595, the Spanish supported Tyrone's Irish rebellion against the English.

- Further Spanish invasion attempts, in 1596 and 1597, were wrecked by storms.

- In 1599, another fleet assembled to attack England, but was dispersed to deal with the Dutch. Spanish troops who had landed in Ireland in 1601 were stranded by storms and surrendered.

- James I made peace with Spain by the Treaty of London (1604).

(b) Explain how the results of this war affected England. (10)

- Politically, England grew in confidence. She became established as a major European power as her prestige and reputation increased.

- Elizabeth I and her government extended their influence.

- Victory fostered early feelings of national pride and Elizabeth I became a living legend.

- England had successfully championed the cause of European Protestantism.

- The growth of England's overseas empire was stimulated. Trade began to expand and there were notable economic gains.

- An interest in ships and ship-building was fostered, as England began to regard her navy as important in both military and economic terms.

7. (a) Describe the main reasons why the Duke of Monmouth rebelled in 1685. (20)

- James Scott, Duke of Monmouth, eldest illegitimate son of Charles II, led a rebellion making a bid for the English crown in June 1685.

- Monmouth claimed to have secret documents proving that he was the legal heir to Charles II.

- Monmouth exploited a story that Charles II, before his marriage to Catherine of Braganza, had been secretly married to Lucy Walter, Monmouth's mother, Indeed, rumours of this were so strong that Charles II had to make a formal denial in 1679.

- He traded on his supposed popularity in England after military successes in the Netherlands in 1672–1674.

- As a Protestant, Monmouth hoped for support to keep the Roman Catholic Duke of York from the throne.

- His own hatred of Roman Catholics gave him further reason to plot.

- The Exclusion Bills (1679–1681) encouraged Monmouth to press forward. The Exclusionists, led by Shaftesbury, supported Monmouth as Charles II's Protestant son. They wanted him proclaimed legitimate so that he could take the throne to the exclusion of Catholic James.

- After the Popish Plot of Tutus Oates (1678) and with the anti-Roman Catholic riots of the time, Monmouth felt that he had a great opportunity to acquire power.

(b) Explain how much of a threat this rebellion was to the government of the time. (10)

- For a short time in June 1685, when Monmouth and his supporters landed at Lyme Regis and he was proclaimed king at Taunton, he appeared to pose a threat to the government.

- In reality, Monmouth was never a problem. His followers were disorganised and poorly equipped. They lacked military skill and the uprising was easily crushed at the Battle of Sedgemoor.

- Monmouth was a poor leader. His campaign lacked purpose, direction and widespread, popular backing.

- Monmouth's execution removed any future long-term threat to James II.

- The harsh treatment of the rebels by Judge Jeffreys and his Bloody Assizes crushed any threats and deterred any further rebellions for Monmouth's cause.

- The earlier defeat of the Exclusion Bills suggested that Parliament supported James II, despite his Catholicism, and that Monmouth's claims were little regarded.

8. (a) Describe the main events of the Jacobite Rebellion of 1745. (20)

- Charles Stuart sailed from France and landed on the west coast of Scotland, in July 1745. He expected to receive great support, but only six Scottish clans came to help him.

- In August, Charles raised his standard at Glenfinnan and then captured Edinburgh.

- A government army of 4,000 men went north under General Cope, but was defeated at Prestonpans on 21st September 1745.

- The Jacobites decided to invade England. They marched southwards through Carlisle, Preston and Manchester. They received little support and, in December 1745, at Derby, Charles abandoned his plan to capture London and decided to retreat northwards.

- General Hawley led an army of 8,000 men north, but was defeated at Falkirk in January 1746. The Duke of Cumberland went northwards with an army. The Jacobites retreated towards Inverness.

- The Battle of Culloden was fought on 16th April 1746. The Jacobites were defeated in about 40 minutes, losing over 1,000 soldiers. The government army lost only about 50 men.

- After the battle, Cumberland sent his men to clear the Highlands in an attempt to destroy Jacobitism for ever.

- Charles Stuart eventually escaped to France with the help of Flora MacDonald.

(b) Explain why Charles Stuart failed to overthrow George II. (10)

- The Jacobites were disorganised, lacking a united purpose. There was no unified command and arguments between Murray and O'Sullivan weakened them. Not all Scots supported the rebels.

- They were short of food, weapons and ammunition.

- Charles Stuart did not inspire widespread popular support either in England or in Scotland. Large-scale French help failed to arrive.

- Jacobite links to Roman Catholicism made them unpopular. George II was popular and England wanted peace and prosperity, not rebellion and disorder.

- The Jacobite army was poorly trained and military defeat at Culloden ended 'the rash adventure'.

- After Culloden, Jacobitism was no longer a real threat to the government.

Government and Parliament

1. (a) Describe the main events of Henry VII's work as king in England. (20)

- Henry strengthened himself through his marriage to Elizabeth of York in 1486 by uniting the houses of York and Lancaster.

- Lambert Simnel pretended to be the Earl of Warwick. Henry crushed this rebellion at Stoke (1487).

- Perkin Warbeck claimed to be Richard, Duke of York. Between 1494 and 1498, Warbeck gained the support of Scotland, Burgundy and the German Emperor. Henry crushed the rebels. Warbeck was executed in 1499.

- Henry passed the De Facto Act (1495), stating that anyone who opposed him could be executed as a traitor. He also gained great wealth by collecting taxes harshly through his agents, Empson, Dudley and Morton. By 1509, Henry VII had over £2 million in his treasury.

- Henry developed trade. He passed the Navigation Laws to encourage English shipping, and supported explorers such as John Cabot who discovered Newfoundland in 1497.

- Henry also tried to extend his power in Ireland through Poynings' Law (1494).

- Henry successfully founded a dynasty. Although Arthur died in 1502, his second son, Henry became Henry VIII in 1509.

- Henry created stable government. Through the Statutes of Livery and Maintenance, he limited the power of his 'over-mighty' subjects by banning their private armies and stopping them from corrupting judges.

- He established the Court of Star Chamber, based upon his own special power as king.

(b) Explain how Henry VII's policies served to make England strong. (10)

- Henry's crushing of the two major rebellions strengthened the monarchy, as did his marriage to Elizabeth which united some old enemies.

- His strengthening of royal finance and his development of trade helped to make England strong.

- Henry's strengthening of law and order and his increased control of the nobility also meant more chance of peace and prosperity and thus created a stronger kingdom.

- That Henry VIII came to the throne so peacefully compared to his father, is a sign that Henry VII's work had made England strong by 1509.

2. (a) Describe the main features of Thomas Wolsey's career. (20)

- Wolsey was the son of an Ipswich butcher. He rose to such power as Henry VIII's chief advisor (1509–1529) that he was called *alter rex* (the other king).

- He was a hard worker, earning rapid promotion in Church and state: 1511, Privy Councillor; 1514, Archbishop of York; 1515, Cardinal and Lord Chancellor; 1518, Papal Legate. It is said that Wolsey even thought of becoming Pope.

- Through subsidies and benevolences, Wolsey raised large sums of money for Henry VIII's glorious policies and rich Renaissance court.

- Wolsey strengthened the Courts of Star Chamber, Chancery and Requests.

- He tried to stamp out Church abuses and closed down some of the smaller, corrupt monasteries after 1525.

- Wolsey planned Henry VIII's French campaign of 1512–1513 and tried to increase England's influence abroad.

- In 1518, he achieved a diplomatic triumph, bringing together the Papacy and the rulers of France, the Empire, Burgundy and the Netherlands through the Treaty of London.

- Wolsey set up the splendid meeting of Francis I of France with Henry VIII at the 'Field of the Cloth of Gold' near Calais in June 1520.

- In 1521, as an ally of Emperor Charles V, he organised an ineffective and expensive war against France.

- Wolsey fell from power in 1529 and died at Leicester Abbey in 1530 on his way to London to face his fate – trial and certain execution.

(b) Explain why he fell from power. (10)

- Wolsey was unpopular with the nobility and the people.

- He had become too rich, arrogant and powerful, and had many jealous enemies waiting for him to make a mistake.

- After 1527, Wolsey failed to obtain Clement VII's permission for Henry VIII to divorce Catherine of Aragon. This was the king's greatest wish. Unable to deliver it, Wolsey was doomed.

- Henry discovered that Wolsey had written to the Pope begging him to persuade Henry not to marry Anne Boleyn.

- Wolsey was accused of treason for failing the king. Of humble origin, he had nothing to support him once the king's favour was lost.

3. (a) Describe the main events of Thomas Cromwell's career in government. (20)

- Thomas Cromwell was Henry VIII's chief advisor between 1530 and 1540.

- Of humble origin, he rose rapidly to power, holding many important jobs such as Master of the Rolls (1534) and Lord Great Chamberlain (1539).

- Cromwell was a Protestant reformer who wished to reduce papal power in England.

- He managed the English Reformation, passing a series of important laws. Foremost among these were the Act of Annates (1532), the Restraint of Appeals to Rome (1533) and the Act of Supremacy (1534), by which Henry VIII became 'supreme head' of the new Church of England.

- Cromwell supervised the Dissolution of the Monasteries (1536–1540). Monastic wealth was recorded in the *Valor Ecclesiasticus* (1535), following which Cromwell's agents investigated allegations of corruption or abuse and closed them down.

- About 650 monasteries were destroyed. Because of this, Cromwell is sometimes referred to as *Malleus monachorum* (the Hammer of the Monks).

- Cromwell made Henry VIII rich, although much monastic land and wealth passed to the gentry and aristocracy.

- In 1540, he fell from power after persuading Henry to marry Anne of Cleves whom the king, upon meeting, found unattractive.

- Owing to his power, he was hated by many. Accused of treason, he was sent to the Tower and executed.

(b) Explain what you think was his greatest achievement. (10)

- It might be argued that the Dissolution of the Monasteries was Cromwell's greatest achievement because it had so many far-reaching effects.

- The Dissolution demonstrated that Cromwell was a brilliant administrator, managing such a major project.

- Cromwell's Dissolution generated important social and economic changes, bringing about the largest transfer of land since the Norman Conquest.

- Owing to Cromwell the Tudor gentry prospered, acquiring land and constructing new houses. Many families, such as the Russells of Woburn Abbey, began to build up their estates which were to flourish in the future.

- Cromwell's monastic policy also increased the political power and influence of the Crown.

- Through the Dissolution, Cromwell helped Henry VIII to establish his royal supremacy over the Church.

- Cromwell even produced educational benefits, as schools were eventually set up in some former monastic buildings.

4. (a) Describe the work of William Cecil (Lord Burghley) in his time as the chief minister of Elizabeth I. (20)

- William Cecil, Lord Burghley, was Elizabeth I's loyal chief minister for 40 years from 1558, when appointed Secretary of State, until his death. Elizabeth referred to him as 'my spirit' and trusted him totally.

- He became a lord in 1571 and Lord Treasurer (1572).

- In Parliament, Burghley acted as Elizabeth's spokesman, keeping her in touch with MPs' various moods and concerns.

- Burghley was industrious, paying attention to the smallest details of government. Through Francis Walsingham, he built up an extended spy network to protect Elizabeth from threats.

- In domestic policy, Burghley was careful and cautious. He was concerned to preserve the queen's security, especially from Roman Catholic plots.

- He exposed the Ridolfi Plot (1571), the Throckmorton Plot (1583) and the Babington Plot (1586).

- Burghley was prudent with money. He reduced government spending and introduced many financial reforms to help increase royal revenue.

- He worked hard to improve and extend trade, encouraging exploration to generate business with the New World and the East, through the establishment of companies of merchant adventurers.

- Burghley was watchful in foreign policy, ever concerned with the power of Catholic Spain. Phillip II's Armada came as no surprise to him and he ensured that England's defences were secure against any possible foreign invasion. He knew, too, that war was expensive.

(b) Explain how successful Cecil was in running the government for Elizabeth I. (10)

- Despite the fact that he believed that it was crucial to England for Elizabeth to marry, and was overruled in this matter, Burghley was a successful minister.

- He was industrious and faithful to the state, providing a cool, calm head as an elder statesman, offering steady advice to Elizabeth.

- With Walsingham, he played an important role in maintaining England's and Elizabeth's security.

- He preserved Elizabeth from the threats from Mary, Queen of Scots, finally solving the problem by Mary's execution in 1587.

- Burghley helped Elizabeth control Parliament and co-ordinated the activities of her Privy Council.

- Overall, Burghley was successful because his outlook matched Elizabeth's. He stood for the new Protestant England and the England of expanding trade and commerce.

5. (a) Describe the main quarrels between Elizabeth I and her Parliaments. (20)

- Elizabeth did not see Parliament as being a permanent part of the government and only summoned it ten times during her 45-year reign. Some MPs objected to this approach.

- Parliament was called usually when she wanted to pass laws or raise money. This upset some people who wanted a wider influence in governing the country.

- Elizabeth recognised Parliament's right to discuss matters of state, but forbade their interference in certain areas. There were quarrels because Parliament wanted a greater say in all royal policies.

- Parliament and Elizabeth quarrelled when MPs tried to insist that she marry. Several candidates were pressed upon her, including Philip II of Spain. Elizabeth refused all of them, claiming that she was wedded to her country.

- The problem of the succession was an important subject of further arguments. MPs wished to protect England from Mary, Queen of Scots, Elizabeth's closest living relative.

- Parliament constantly pressed the queen to name an heir. Elizabeth refused, telling them not to meddle. Only in 1603, on her deathbed, did she nominate James VI of Scotland.

- There were quarrels over religion, as when Anthony Cope, in 1587, tried to make some changes to the Prayer Book in the interests of the Puritans. The queen was furious. Cope, with several of his supporters, was arrested and sent to the Tower.

(b) Explain how successful Elizabeth was in managing Parliament. (10)

- Elizabeth was generally successful in managing Parliament because MPs and the queen agreed on two main principles: the maintenance of Protestantism and the defence of England from foreign enemies.

- Elizabeth successfully used Parliament to pass good laws such as those which dealt with the care of the poor (1597–1601).

- Elizabeth was skilful with Parliament. Although there were quarrels and occasionally she ignored them or cleverly delayed decisions, she also flattered them.

- Elizabeth played upon the fact that she was a woman, using her charm to win hearts and minds.

- She controlled her Parliaments, forbidding any notable developments in either their powers or functions.

- Her overall success is suggested by her Golden Speech (1601), when she claimed proudly that she was fortunate to rule with their love.

6. (a) Describe the relations between James I and Charles I and their Parliaments in the period from 1603 to 1642. (20)

- Both James and Charles believed in the Divine Right Theory of Kings, which stated that monarchs were given their right to rule by God. Thus, it was against God to question royal authority. This attitude coloured their dealings with Parliament.

- In 1604, James started badly when Parliament refused to grant a subsidy for the war against Spain. The Addled Parliament (1614) lasted only eight weeks after James failed to obtain financial grants.

- There were quarrels in 1621 over MPs' rights to discuss foreign policy and the proposed marriage of Prince Charles to the Spanish *Infanta*.

- The 1624 Parliament saw the impeachment of Cranfield, the king's treasurer and a grant of money for a war against Spain, which James had opposed.

- Charles did little better. In 1627, forced loans were introduced after arguments with Parliament over taxation.

- Owing to opposition, shown through the Petition of Right (1628) and the Three Resolutions (1629), Charles dismissed Parliament for the next 11 years.

- Relations with both kings were soured by their constant use of favourites.

- During the Period of Personal Rule (1629–1640), would-be MPs were angered by Charles's use of Strafford and Laud and their policies concerning taxation, religion and Scotland.

- Such was the level of hostility to the Crown in April 1640 that Charles abandoned Parliament after only three weeks.

- When recalled in November 1640, Parliament systematically stripped the king of his ministers and their apparatus of royal government.

- Feeling robbed of his rightful powers, Charles declared war on Parliament in August 1642.

(b) Explain how the actions of James I and Charles I affected the history of England in this period. (10)

- In the short term to 1642, the actions of James and Charles led politicians to question certain aspects of royal policies and authority.

- James and Charles had upset the political, religious, economic and military stability of the country.

- Owing to Charles's inflexibility, civil war was reluctantly seen by some as the only realistic way to achieve a political settlement.

- In the longer term, royal policies led to the execution of a king and the introduction of a political experiment without monarchy.

- Political and religious thinking were advanced as men developed new concepts of Church and state.

7. (a) Describe the main features of Oliver Cromwell's period of power from 1649 to 1658. (20)

- After Charles I's execution, England faced many threats. Oliver Cromwell seized the initiative and made himself secure.

- In 1649, Cromwell crushed Irish rebellions at Drogheda and Wexford. He then defeated the Scots at Dunbar (1650) and overcame a royalist bid for power at the Battle of Worcester (1651).

- Cromwell established himself as Lord Protector by 1653, having dissolved the Rump Parliament and the Parliament of the Saints. Despite wishing to co-operate with Parliament, the army remained the basis of his authority.

- Cromwell began domestic reforms to build a 'godly commonwealth'. In private, people could worship freely, but laws were introduced to make England's way of life more Puritan.

- Theatres and dancing were banned, as were swearing, drinking and even Christmas celebrations (1652). There were long sermons in Puritan chapels.

- In 1655, he divided England into 11 military districts, each commanded by a Major General whose job was to raise taxes, keep order and 'promote godliness and virtue'. A 10% tax was introduced to raise a militia force for each district.

- In foreign policy, Cromwell maintained England's interests and protected his regime. He made peace with the Dutch (1654) and took Jamaica in a war against Spain.

- To beat the Spanish in Europe, he allied with France. A commercial treaty with Sweden (1656) boosted England's trading rights in the Baltic.

- Although Cromwell refused the Crown, he was confirmed as Lord Protector in a magnificent ceremony in 1657. His death in 1658 brought in his son, Richard, who was unable to continue his father's policies.

(b) Explain how far you think Cromwell was a success. (10)

- In the short term, Cromwell was successful. He destroyed his enemies both at home and abroad and established a new way of governing England.

- In religious matters, he worked towards the creation of his Puritan ideal, although this was not fully established.

- Perhaps Cromwell was less successful in the longer term. In the 1660s, both monarchy and Anglicanism were re-established as important pillars of the state.

- On the other hand, Cromwell had generated a situation where no future monarch could do as he pleased.

- More attention was paid to the rights and privileges of Parliament. It may be said that Cromwell was successful in advancing the rights and liberties of Englishmen.

8. (a) Describe the main developments in the relationship between the Crown and Parliament in the period 1660–1688. (20)

- 1660–1688 saw the slow development of co-operation rather than confrontation between Crown and Parliament.

- The Convention Parliament (1660) and the Cavalier Parliament (1661–1679) were royalist and supported Charles II. With Parliament largely on his side, Charles II was able to restore many of the monarchy's rights.

- After 1660, two main political groups emerged. The Whigs, who believed that royal power should be limited, and the Tories, many of whom supported the idea of the Divine Right of Kings and stood firmly by the Church of England. Thus, Charles had to tread carefully in all he did.

- In religious matters, Charles worked with Parliament to strengthen the Church of England through the Clarendon Code (1661–1665).

- Parliament monitored royal policies and Charles's Declaration of Indulgence (1672), through which Roman Catholics and dissenters received greater religious freedom, was answered by the Test Act (1673), requiring all government officials to take a Protestant oath.

- Parliament rallied to the monarchy after the Popish Plot (1678), and the failure of the Exclusion Bills (1679–1681) suggested that MPs were keen to maintain the legitimate succession, even with the prospect of a Catholic ruler.

- However, the Rye House Plot (1683) dented the relationship between Crown and MPs. Charles II called no further Parliaments.

- Charles II kept control of foreign policy and did not always tell Parliament the whole truth. In 1670, he made the Treaty of Dover with Louis XIV, in which he secretly promised to become a Roman Catholic if the French would pay him a large subsidy. This money would have given the king more independence from Parliament.

- Parliament welcomed James II in 1685. However, tensions grew as the king developed his pro-Catholic policies and he was eventually deposed in 1688.

(b) Explain how the power of Parliament changed during this time. (10)

- The power of Parliament grew from 1660 to 1688.

- Kings now had to work with Parliament. Charles II showed what could be achieved by co-operation.

- James II's reign illustrated the consequences of a monarch opposing Parliamentary wishes.

- The Glorious Revolution (1688) demonstrated Parliament's ability to control royal power and to impose a mechanism of checks and balances upon kingly rule.

- The power of Parliament gradually developed, creating the beginnings of the Constitutional Monarchy which we have in Britain today.

9. (a) Describe the main reasons for the passing of the Act of Union (1707). (20)

- By 1707, relations between England and Scotland were deteriorating, so Anne's government wanted to sort out the situation in case Scotland were to ally with England's enemies.

- In political terms, Scotland resented being dominated by England. Many Scots disliked the Act of Settlement barring James Edward Stuart from the English throne. Scotland wanted the right to choose its own ruler.

- Some members of the Scottish parliament received English bribes to vote in favour of a union.

- England hoped for more control over Scotland through a union of the two parliaments, as all new laws would be made by the parliament in Westminster.

- There were foreign policy differences. Scotland did not support England's declaration of war on France in 1702.

- Anne's government was worried about the possibility of a Scottish alliance with Louis XIV and felt threatened. Anglo-Scottish union would prevent this.

- There were economic tensions as Scotland's merchants were banned from trading with England's colonies. Scotland felt excluded from England's growing commercial success.

- Scotland's main exports to England were cattle, linens and coal. In 1705, England threatened to ban these unless there were talks about a union.

- Many English MPs believed that a union would strengthen England. Scottish opposition would be removed, allowing the two countries more chance of co-operating to settle their differences.

(b) Explain how the passing of this Act affected the history of the United Kingdom. (10)

- In the short term, the Union led to a reduction of Anglo-Scottish tensions, although not all difficulties were overcome, as shown by the Jacobite Rebellions of 1715 and 1745.

- In the longer term, the Union led to the making of the United Kingdom. In 1707, Great Britain was created. This lasted until the Act of Union with Ireland (1801) to make the United Kingdom of Great Britain and Ireland.

- Only in 1998 was the Scottish Parliament re-established, in line with Scotland's wishes under a process of devolution.

- Overall, the Union of 1707 helped to create a strong political and economic state which played a major role in the world until influence began to decline in the years after 1945.

10. (a) Describe the main achievements of Sir Robert Walpole. (20)

- The Spanish Succession War (1702–1713) left the country in debt. Walpole set up a Sinking Fund (1717) to reduce this. The fund cut the National Debt by £12.8 million.

- In 1720, England was rocked by the South Sea Bubble crisis. The government was blamed. Walpole restored confidence and financial order to the government.

- Walpole developed cabinet government and took charge of cabinet meetings.

- He generated a system of politics based on patronage. Walpole offered MPs rewards, like positions in government, the Church and the army, as well as special trade privileges. To some he gave money. Walpole claimed that 'Every man has his price'. In return for patronage, MPs promised Walpole support in the Commons. Walpole had fashioned a new mechanism of politics.

- He became Prime Minister and is said to be England's first Prime Minister.

- As a favourite of Princess Caroline, Walpole survived George I's death (1727). New kings usually brought in fresh ministers, but Caroline persuaded George II to keep him. Walpole claimed that he 'had the right sow by the ear', meaning that he was successful because he had the queen's support.

(b) Explain why he fell from power in 1742. (10)

- Opposition grew to his peaceful foreign policy. Walpole wanted peace for trade to flourish, but some claimed that England was losing influence abroad.

- In 1739, Walpole had to go to war against Spain, so his peace policy was shattered. This weakened him politically.

- In 1733, Walpole tried to raise money by introducing an Excise Bill to tax wine and tobacco. There was great opposition and the Bill was withdrawn. Walpole's status was damaged.

- Queen Caroline died in 1737, removing one of his supporters when he was facing increasing opposition. This further weakened him.

- Walpole was satirised in the press and the theatre by writers such as John Gay and Henry Fielding.

- William Pitt's brilliant attacks in the Commons over Walpole's poor handling of the war, forced his resignation in February 1742.

Religion

1. (a) Describe the main features of the Church in England before the Reformation. (20)

- The pre-Reformation Church in England was part of the wider Roman Catholic Church controlled by the Pope in Rome.

- The fundamental beliefs of the Christian faith were the same as in Europe and elsewhere, but England had a degree of independence from Rome owing to her island status.

- The English Church was organised into two provinces, each looked after by archbishops, in Canterbury and York. Below them came the bishops, each in charge of a diocese.

- Dioceses were divided into archdeaconries consisting of several rural deaneries. A rural deanery was a collection of parishes. Each parish constituted the equivalent to a village.

- People looked to the Church for salvation. Fear of damnation in Hell, for following a sinful life, was very real.

- Each parish had a church with a priest to care for the spiritual needs of his people. Priests christened, married and buried their parishioners. Good priests also taught the scriptures, said Mass, tended the sick and troubled and taught some of the brighter children.

- The village church was the centre of social life, used for sports, meetings and celebrations on Saints' Days and festivals.

- There were monasteries and convents, where men and women shut themselves off from the world to follow a life of prayer, poverty, chastity and obedience.

- Friars, like the Franciscans and Dominicans, travelled the country preaching and begging.

(b) Explain why the condition of the Church led many people to seek religious change. (10)

- Many people wanted religious change owing to the abuses, corruption and failures within the Church as some men and women fell below the clerical ideal.

- Some priests shamed themselves. They married or had girlfriends; they failed to say their services or look after their parishes. Some were drunkards.

- Ordinary people came to resent the easy life of some priests and feelings of anti-clericalism grew.

- Many monasteries failed in their original purpose. Monks became rich and lazy, acquiring large amounts of land and treasure.

- Some churchmen worked in royal government, not leading religious lives.

- Reforming ideas, such as those of Luther, spread to England.

- The Renaissance produced new thinking and led people to be critical of what was wrong and to seek change.

2. (a) Describe the main stages of Henry VIII's reformation of the Church. (20)

- After Henry VIII had failed to obtain an annulment of his marriage to Catherine of Aragon, he decided to achieve this by making his own Church.

- Henry's reformation of the English Church was accomplished by passing a series of laws in Parliament, cutting back papal power and influence in England.

- The Act of Annates (1532), confirmed in the following year, stopped all payment of money to Rome.

- An Act in Restraint of Appeals (1533) forbade all appeals to Rome and asserted that Henry VIII had supreme authority in all temporal and spiritual matters.

- The 1534 Act of Supremacy made Henry VIII 'Supreme Head' of the English Church. Papal authority was gone.

- A Treason Act (1534) declared that any person denying Henry's position as Head of the Church could be tried for treason.

- Another Act granted Henry VIII the first year's income from dioceses and all benefices, and one tenth of the annual income thereafter. This law was administered by the Court of First Fruits and Tenths, established in 1540.

- 1536–1540 saw laws for the Dissolution of the Monasteries.

- Through these laws, Henry VIII made the break from Rome. The Church *in* England became the Church *of* England.

- Up to 1536, Henry's new laws had entailed little alteration to the teachings or practices of the Church. Changes in doctrine came about through the Ten Articles (1536) and the Six Articles (1539).

(b) Explain why Henry was able to change the Church so quickly. (10)

- The Roman Catholic Church was unpopular in England. People hated paying taxes to the Pope.

- The wishes of many in England coincided with Henry's own desires.

- Many disliked the clergy and there was a growing sense of anti-clericalism.

- Laymen regarded nuns and monks as having an easy life. They saw the laziness, the luxury and the corruption and they wanted, partly through jealousy, to be rid of them.

- Reformers, like Martin Luther, had broken away from Rome, providing an example for Henry VIII to follow.

- As the result of the Renaissance, it became easier to criticise and change institutions such as the Church.

3. (a) Describe the most important religious changes which occurred in the reign of Edward VI. (20)

- Edward VI's advisers, Somerset and Northumberland, wanted to develop the Reformation by setting down clearly the doctrines of the new English Protestant Church.

- In 1549, the Act of Uniformity imposed worship across England from a new Prayer Book, in English. This was reinforced by a second English Prayer Book in 1552.

- Transubstantiation was denied. The Mass was replaced by Holy Communion, a service in remembrance of the Last Supper.

- The forms of baptisms, weddings and funerals were also laid down.

- Chantries were abolished in 1547, their money and property passing to the Crown.

- In 1553, the 42 Articles of Religion specified the doctrines of the English Church.

- Medieval Guilds, often associated with the Virgin Mary, were abolished.

- Changes took place within churches. Images and statues were banned; plain lights replaced stained-glass and walls were whitewashed to cover bright wall-paintings. Often in their place, were tablets bearing texts such as the Lord's Prayer or the Creed.

- Services became simpler with less ritual and more emphasis on Bible reading and preaching.

- Stone altars were replaced by simple, wooden tables. Priests were referred to as ministers and told to dress in simple clothes. They were permitted to marry and have children.

(b) Explain how Edward's changes affected the future of religion up to 1558. (10)

- Edward's changes helped the establishment of English Protantism and took the Church away from Rome.

- Edward laid the foundations of a Church that Mary I was determined to destroy. His work thus set in motion intense religious strife.

- The religious upheavals following Edward's reforms established the idea, for a time, that the religion of the state should be that of the current monarch.

- Between 1553 and 1558, Mary swept away all Edward's work, returning the English Church to Rome through the Counter-Reformation.

- On the other hand, Protestantism was so deeply entrenched that many refused to obey Mary and died at the stake as Protestant martyrs.

- Mary's cruelty in re-establishing Catholicism ironically served to strengthen the very Church she wished to destroy, so traces of Edward's changes survived for Elizabeth to build on after 1558.

4. (a) Describe the main features of the Elizabethan Church Settlement of 1559. (20)

- The Act of Supremacy (1559) made Elizabeth I 'Supreme Governor' of the Church. She had once more made the monarch head of the Church of England.

- The Act of Uniformity (1559) brought many changes.

- A new English Prayer Book was issued, based on those of 1549 and 1552. All services were to be in English, not Latin; priests had to keep registers of all births, deaths and marriages and an English Bible was to be provided for all, in every church.

- The rules of 1549, concerning the vestments worn by priests, were also re-introduced.

- Clergy were made to use the new Prayer Book; any who refused were removed from office.

- Sunday attendance at church became compulsory. Failure to obey this led to fines, known as recusancy fines.

- The 1559 Settlement was a compromise and Elizabeth only punished religious extremists.

- Her amalgamation of the 1549 and 1552 Prayer Books provided a broad range for the interpretation of religious doctrines. For example, in the Holy Communion Service, it was possible to believe that the bread and wine became the actual body and blood of Christ; that this happened only for those who truly believed in Him, or that they simply commemorated Christ's presence.

- Elizabeth appointed bishops and archbishops with moderate Protestant ideas.

- The Settlement represented a 'middle way' through which the queen wanted to satisfy the majority of her subjects.

(b) Explain why Elizabeth wanted to make such a settlement. (10)

- Elizabeth made a compromise settlement because she wanted to try to end the religious strife between Catholics, Anglicans and Puritans which was tearing her kingdom and weakening it.

- She thought that compromise would bring religious unity which, in turn, would lead to political unity and, thus, strength.

- Elizabeth was moderate, aiming to avoid conflict between extreme Catholicism and strict Puritanism.

- She did not wish to 'make windows into men's souls'. As long as people attended church services and obeyed her laws, she did not enquire too deeply into their actual religious beliefs.

- Her aim was a settlement acceptable to the majority of her people.

5. (a) Describe the position of Puritans and Roman Catholics during the reign of Elizabeth I. (20)

- Hard-line Puritans and Roman Catholic extremists never accepted the 1559 Church Settlement and posed a threat throughout Elizabeth's reign.

- Catholics and Puritans felt that the Settlement made them second-class citizens. Officially, they were not allowed to practise their religions and were fined for non-attendance at Anglican churches.

- In practice, the situation was not so bad. The Settlement was loosely administered and only extremists like John Gerrard and Edmund Campion, who paraded their religion, were persecuted.

- Most Catholics kept out of trouble, especially after 1570 when Elizabeth was excommunicated.

- Catholics were viewed as being disloyal to the state owing to their links with foreign powers such as Spain.

- In reality, most Catholics and Puritans, if not actually content, went to Anglican services to avoid recusancy fines and lived quiet lives as honest Englishmen. Catholics remained loyal to the Pope in religion, but loyal to Elizabeth in politics.

- Mass was said behind closed doors and Puritans had secret prayer meetings.

- Some Catholics refused to accept Elizabeth as queen, as the Pope had not recognised Henry VIII's marriage to Anne Boleyn.

- Many Puritans realised they were better off with Elizabeth than with a Catholic monarch and that their position under the Church of England was not as bad as it could be.

(b) Explain how Puritans and Roman Catholics tried to improve their religious position within England. (10)

- Catholic extremists tried to improve their position through the Northern Rebellion (1569), the Ridolfi Plot (1571), the Throckmorton Plot (1583) and the Babington Plot (1586). Extremist Catholics favoured Mary, Queen of Scots as ruler.

- Jesuit priests were active during the 1580s, celebrating Mass and trying to win converts.

- Puritans tried to make religious changes through Parliament, with little success as Elizabeth kept a firm control over MPs.

- Throughout the 1570s and 1580s, Puritans turned to 'prophesyings', meeting together for prayer and discussion.

- Presbyterianism developed during the 1580s, with Bible study, prayer groups and discussion of the whole Church structure. They questioned the utility of bishops.

- Extreme Puritans expressed their ideas through lectures, such as those by Thomas Cartwright at Cambridge (1570) and the publication of their own Prayer Book in 1574.

6. (a) Describe the main features of Archbishop Laud's religious policies. (20)

- After his appointment as Archbishop of Canterbury in 1633, Laud was determined to bring uniformity to the Church. He wanted all parishes to worship in the same way.

- He demanded elaborate services with ceremony and symbolism. He wanted 'high-church' practices with choirs, organs, processions and candles. He thought this helped to lead the mind to God. Laud believed in 'the beauty of holiness'.

- Stone altars were reintroduced and placed at the east end of churches, protected by altar rails. Laud believed in the Mystery of the Sacrament; for him, the Holy Communion was the most important aspect of worship.

- Laud demanded that sermons should be on the subject of obedience to God, the king and the Church, and be delivered without opinion.

- He increased the collection of tithes, to strengthen the Church through raising its income.

- After 1637, Laud tried (and failed) to enforce his version of English Protestantism in Scotland against the Presbyterians.

- Laud hated Catholics and Puritans. He persecuted any who opposed him, such as Prynne, Burton and Bastwick in 1637.

- Laud worked hard in state matters. He demanded a strong clergy to help in government. He encouraged his ministers to support the Divine Right of Kings theory.

- Laud sought power for the king and co-operated with Strafford. The two men were united in their prime purpose to create a strong monarchy.

- Laud used the Court of High Commission to enforce his will. This was a prerogative court, equivalent to the Star Chamber.

(b) Explain how successful you believe Laud was in achieving his goals. (10)

- Laud was successful in the short term, in England, up to about 1637, when his ideas were carried through. By the late 1630s, opposition was growing.

- He failed in Scotland (1637–1640). His religious policies led to the Prayer Book riots in Edinburgh, the strengthening of Presbyterianism through the National Covenant (1638) and, ultimately, to the Bishops' Wars (1639–1640).

- In political terms, Laud failed in England after 1640 when the Long Parliament swept away the religious apparatus of the Period of Personal Rule.

- In the longer term, however, Laud was perhaps not a total failure. In many Anglican churches today, 'high-church' practices still take place and 'the beauty of holiness' continues.

7. (a) Describe the religious opinions and influences of the Puritans between 1603 and 1649. (20)

- Puritans were extreme Protestants who wished to 'purify' the Church. They wanted simple services in plain chapels, regarding ceremony and ornaments as Catholic and as distractions to true worship.

- There were many sorts of Puritanism, such as Presbyterianism in Scotland.

- Some Puritans wished to dispose of bishops and priests, believing that Man's personal relationship with God did not need interference from clergy.

- Puritans emphasised Bible study and preaching. They spread their ideas through pamphlets.

- Puritans liked to dress simply, be frugal in their habits, work hard and live Godly lives each day. They objected to swearing, drinking and dancing.

- They thought they were chosen by God to fight against sin.

- Puritans tried to increase their influence through the Millenary Petition (1603) and the debates during the Hampton Court Conference (1604).

- There was a large Puritan element among the opposition to James I in Parliament.

- During the Period of Personal Rule, Puritan books and pamphlets increasingly alienated them from Charles I.

- Puritans in the Long Parliament tried to increase their power through the Nineteen Propositions (1642).

- Puritan influence grew as Cromwell gained importance after about 1644. Fairfax and Cromwell spread Puritan ideas throughout the New Model Army, which saw itself as fighting to do God's will.

- In 1645, a Puritan Directory of Worship replaced the Prayer Book.

- During the Civil War, Puritan influences grew through groups like the Fifth Monarchy Men, Levellers and Independents. The majority of the regicides were Puritan.

(b) Explain the most important consequences of their beliefs. (10)

- Puritan attempts to win power at the start of James's reign led to a backlash against them by the king's bishops.

- Following their constant attacks on him, Laud opposed Puritans throughout the 1630s.

- Owing to increasing Puritan support for the opposition to Charles I, a major consequence of their beliefs was Cromwell's rise, leading to the Puritan experiment of the Commonwealth and Protectorate.

- In the longer term, a further consequence was the re-establishment of the Church of England in the 1660s after the unpopularity of a Puritan government.

- There was a widening of theology with the arrival of the new beliefs of various puritan groups.

8. (a) Describe how and why John Bunyan was persecuted. (20)

- Despite the promises made in the Declaration of Breda (1660), Charles II gave little support to religious freedoms. Thus, Bunyan (1628–1688) suffered as a dissenter.

- After three years in the parliamentary army, Bunyan returned to Bedford to resume his trade as a tinker. He began serious Bible study, which stimulated his desire to preach Puritan beliefs.

- By 1655, he had joined a religious set founded by John Gifford. In 1656, Bunyan began to preach without a licence.

- His popularity grew and he became closely associated with the growth of local Puritanism. Bunyan showed that no special education was necessary and that anyone with a calling could preach God's Word.

- Bunyan was persecuted because of his simple message that the Bible was the source of all Truth and that salvation came through faith in Christ, rather than by good works alone.

- The authorities were frightened. Bunyan was seen as a threat by the local magistrates. On the order of Sir Francis Wingate, he was imprisoned after preaching at Lower Samsall.

- Bunyan was accused of breaking the 1593 Conventicle Act, which forbade Puritan gatherings. However, he refused to stop preaching and was jailed for three months (1660). After further refusals to conform, Bunyan spent the next 12 years in Bedford prison, apart from a short break in 1665.

(b) Explain whether Bunyan was strengthened or weakened by this persecution. (10)

- Far from being cast down into despair, Bunyan was strengthened by his persecution.

- While in Bedford Prison, he preached to fellow inmates and wrote Puritan books, such as *Grace Abounding* (1666).

- After his release, he continued his work as Preacher to the Non-Conformist Church in Bedford.

- Bunyan also spread his message to large crowds in London.

- Arrested again in 1675 and imprisoned for six months, Bunyan used the time to write *The Pilgrim's Progress* published in 1678. This tells the story of Christian (Bunyan) successfully overcoming many hardships in order to reach the Celestial City (Heaven).

- Over 100,000 copies were sold in Bunyan's lifetime, and the book became second only to the Bible in popularity over the next 300 years. Such was Bunyan's strength, faith and success, despite persecution.

Social History

1. (a) Describe the enclosure movement of the 16th century. (20)

- English wool fetched high prices in the Flemish weaving towns. This led to an increase in sheep farming in England, as such profits outstripped those from arable cultivation.

- To support the extra sheep, more enclosure was required. The extent of enclosure varied across the country, but was extensive in East Anglia.

- Enclosure meant putting hedges and fences around land that had once been open fields, commons or waste.

- Land was divided into fields and closes, passing into the private ownership of the aristocracy or gentry.

- One shepherd could look after hundreds of sheep, whereas it took many labourers to grow the same value of corn. These extra men were now redundant in the villages.

- Sir Thomas More commented that sheep were eating men as unemployed labourers were driven from the countryside.

- There were outbreaks of rioting and protest by those whose livelihoods were threatened. Fences and hedges were broken down.

- In some areas, magistrates were sympathetic to the protesters and punishments were not usually harsh. However, in 1549, the government faced protests in 23 separate counties.

- A major rebellion of that year, partly against enclosure, was that of Robert Kett in Norfolk. This was ruthlessly crushed and Kett was hanged from the walls of Norwich Castle.

(b) Explain the effects of enclosure on both the rich and the poor of the time. (10)

- Aristocrats and gentry, owning large flocks of sheep, benefited by increased profits from the sale of the extra wool in Flanders.

- The government, although at first cautious of enclosure, also gained. Enclosure stimulated the growth of the woollen industry. More wool was exported through the 'staple' in Calais. The government profited from the increased revenue from the taxes on such exports.

- Wool merchants grew wealthier as their trade developed.

- The poor and their families suffered through the growth of rural unemployment. Many were reduced to poverty, begging, or occasional casual labour.

- With the enclosure of many commons and wastes, on which poorer villagers had eked out a meagre existence, rural suffering increased.

2. (a) Describe the main features of the wool trade in the 16th century. (20)

- The woollen industry was England's most important trade in the 16th century. Throughout Europe, English wool was famous for its high quality.

- There was an abundance of sheep, mainly in the West Country, Kent, the Midlands, East Anglia and Yorkshire.

- Trade was organised through the putting-out system, where merchants put out raw material to be made up in workers' homes. Men, women and children were all involved in the various stages of converting wool into cloth.

- Some workers were dependent on these wages to get them through the week.

- There were even 'factories', such as that run by William Stumpe at Osney Abbey in Oxford, where several looms had been installed by 1546.

- The trade was helped by the immigration of Flemish weavers.

- Merchants then sold the cloth in London at Bakewell Hall, which became the scene of a weekly market for material brought in from all over the country.

- There were regional cloth markets in towns such as Norwich, Bristol, York and Coventry.

- Woollen cloth was then exported to Europe to be finished in Flanders. Wool from West Yorkshire went to the Baltic. West-Country cloth was exported to France and Spain. By 1550, woollen cloth accounted for 80% of England's total exports.

- After a period of expansion, the wool trade by 1600 had grown beyond the guilds and the local economy, to become a wholesale business run by men who understood industrial competition.

(b) Explain how the trade in wool benefited England during this time. (10)

- The country profited from the increase in trade. The monarchy gained increasing revenue from the taxes on wool.

- A strong merchant class emerged which helped to develop England's economy. There was a growth in capitalist enterprise and business practice.

- New national and international patterns of trade were created and developed to be extended in later centuries as England found her place in the commercial network.

- Technological progress was stimulated.

- There were even benefits to architecture and the building trades with the demand for houses for the rich wool merchants.

- Through the wool trade might be seen the beginnings of the various elements of England's future economic greatness.

3. (a) Describe the main features of overseas trade in the period 1500–1750. (20)

- With the growth of England's domestic economy, overseas trade expanded between 1500 and 1750.

- New trade patterns were established. London merchants learnt how to finish their cloth for export to the Netherlands and France.

- Merchant adventurers developed new markets. After 1600, the East India Company broke the Dutch monopoly on the spice trade and expanded its operations to India itself.

- The growth of ports like London, Bristol and Liverpool further stimulated trade.

- By 1750, England was trading with its 13 North-American colonies, Newfoundland, the Caribbean, the East Indies and the West African coast.

- A so-called 'Triangular Trade' pattern evolved. British merchants carried manufactured goods to Africa, exchanging them for slaves. Slaves were shipped for sale to the plantations of the Americas. Produce from the plantations was then exported to Britain.

- Commerce varied. Imports included wine, sugar, tea, coffee, spirits, furs, silks and raw materials like cotton. Exports initially comprised wool, but widened to embrace tin, lead, coal, salt, iron and pottery. Colonial produce, such as tobacco, sugar and Indian calicoes, was re-exported from England.

- Around 1500, English trade was limited mainly to the North Sea and Europe's Atlantic Coast; by 1750, it was global.

(b) Explain how and why the governments of the time tried to encourage the development of overseas trade. (10)

- Commercial growth was fostered through organisations like the East India Company (1600), the Hudson Bay Company (1670) and the Royal Africa Company (1672), all of which received royal patronage.

- The expansion of overseas trade became a major concern for government ministers.

- Wars were fought largely in the interests of trade and of gaining new colonies through peace treaties, such as Utrecht (1713) and Aix-la-Chapelle (1748). More colonies led to an extension of global trade links.

- Possession of colonies created the beginnings of the Empire. This, in turn, generated political, economic and military power over commercial rivals like the French and Dutch.

- There were cultural gains, as the seeds were sown enabling British ideas to flourish throughout the globe.

- Successive governments were keen to encourage overseas trade to reap the financial benefits of economic growth. Between 1700 and 1731, imports rose by 27%, exports by 17%.

4. (a) Describe the main details of life at Court in the reign of Charles I. (20)

- Charles I maintained a rich Court life with Catholic influences. He had married Henrietta-Maria, a Catholic. She introduced a group of Catholic chaplains and ladies-in-waiting.

- Henrietta established a Catholic chapel. She surrounded Charles with Catholic advisers and sympathisers.

- Although not a Catholic, Charles introduced High-Anglican rituals to his Court chapels, supporting Laud in his love of the 'beauty of holiness'.

- Charles believed passionately in the Divine Right Theory, convinced that his power came directly from God. He stood aloof from his people. This feeling was supported by his courtiers.

- Rich architecture featured in Court life. Charles employed Inigo Jones to complete the Queen's House at Greenwich (1630–1635) for Henrietta. He also finished the Banqueting House in Whitehall, although the scheme to build a huge palace there went unfinished.

- Charles spent large sums of money on works of art by Titian, Raphael and Van Dyck. His art collection was among the best in England.

- Court entertainments, like masques, had a political function to show the virtues of a strong monarchy which prevented England from falling into chaos. Masques controlled the image of royalty, presenting the king almost as a Christ-like saviour.

- There were also many concerts, balls and banquets held in the king's honour, all of which glorified the monarchy.

- The Court circle comprised a small group, centred on the king and seen as Catholic, absolutist and corrupt. Those 'in' with Charles seemed to exist in a dream world, isolated from ordinary people.

(b) Explain how some features of Court life might have led people to oppose Charles I in 1642. (10)

- The arts – drama, painting and architecture – appeared to embody royal power and tyranny. It was art for absolutism which upset Parliamentarians.

- The immorality, favouritism, corruption and drunkenness of the urban Court dismayed those of the Country party, who saw themselves as rural, honest, sober, moral and clean-living.

- The Court represented oppression. Charles's opposition demanded freedom and political privileges.

- Court life seemed to favour Catholicism, which upset Protestant opponents of the king.

- Court culture appeared remote and isolated from ordinary men. The king had cut himself off from his people who resented this, arguing that he had fallen into the grip of 'evil counsellors', who had to be removed.

5. (a) Describe the main details of the Elizabethan Poor Law system. (20)

- Elizabeth's Poor Law system was set out in a series of laws of 1563, 1572, 1576 and 1597, finally drawn together in the Great Poor Law of 1601.

- The poor were classified into two groups: the deserving poor and the idle poor.

- Each parish had to elect annually two Overseers of the Poor, responsible to the local Justice of the Peace.

- These Overseers collected money, known as the Poor Rate, from the rich. This cash was used to help the poor.

- Extra money from local charities could be added to the Poor Rate. Some towns assisted the poor with money collected from rents.

- If the parish had a poorhouse, the deserving poor received help there in the form of indoor relief. Where no poorhouse existed, outdoor relief in their own homes was offered to paupers.

- The idle poor consisted of those who, although fit and healthy, did not work through laziness.

- The law regarded the idle poor as undeserving of charity and as a threat to the social order. They were whipped and returned to the parish of their birth.

- Constant failure to work by the idle poor could result in their being sent to a House of Correction. Here, inmates were forced to work or whipped. Some were even executed for persistent idleness.

(b) Explain why Elizabeth I's Poor Laws are important. (10)

- Elizabeth's 1601 law rationalised earlier schemes on a national scale. The Poor Laws represent an important step in the organisation of proper care for the poor by the state at public expense.

- The system was important for the authorities as a means of social control. Beggars were monitored in order to prevent social unrest. Through the Poor Laws, law and order were maintained.

- The movement of vagrants was regulated so that no parish was overwhelmed by those from other places.

- The government was able to have some effect on the problem of rising unemployment by preventing some people from becoming beggars who might afterwards be a social nuisance.

- The Poor Rate became the basis of all later local taxation within a parish.

- Elizabeth's laws established a method of poor relief which lasted until the 19th century.

6. (a) Describe the main features of life in the countryside during the first half of the 18th century. (20)

- About 80% of people lived in the countryside. Life centred on the village community with its fields, commons, woodlands and wastes.

- There were many ranks of rural society. Aristocracy and gentry lived in country houses on their estates, at least for part of the year. There were wealthy tenant farmers, smaller farmers, labourers and cottagers.

- The squire and the rector were the two most important village inhabitants. The squire owned lots of land and acted as the local magistrate. The rector looked after his church and parishioners, cultivated his glebe and collected his tithes.

- Much land was farmed with large, open fields (300–400 acres) divided into strips which farmers and peasants rented from the lord of the manor.

- In most villages, agriculture followed its regular annual course: autumn ploughing and sowing of winter wheat; hedging and ditching during winter; spring ploughing and sowing; harvesting hay in July and corn in August or September.

- Farming was a co-operative affair. Poorer villagers clubbed together to make up plough teams and everyone helped with the harvest.

- Villagers had the right to graze a few animals or keep ducks or geese on the common.

- For the lower orders, life was hard.

- Some villages were enclosed. Hedges were planted and the strips were divided into smaller fields. Commons were fenced off and natural woodland was often replaced by neat plantations.

(b) Explain how and why country life was changing during this period. (10)

- The population grew steadily.

- The landscape altered as villages were enclosed, producing a new patchwork-quilt effect of field patterns. Many new farmsteads appeared, away from the village.

- Agricultural yields increased through the greater use of fertilisers, a more scientific approach to farming and the introduction of new crop rotations.

- Production also grew owing to the increasing use of new machinery. Jethro Tull invented his seed drill (c.1701) and his horse hoe (c.1714).

- Aristocrats like Coke of Holkham and Viscount Townshend at Rainham actively promoted new methods such as improved crop rotations.

- Land-use changed with the spread of fodder crops and forage plants, such as turnips and sainfoin.

- The quality of animals improved owing to selective breeding by men like Robert Bakewell.

General Topics

1. (a) Describe the main features of the lives of women in the period from about 1700 to 1750. (20)

- Gender determined particular roles for women. A woman's life also depended on her status.

- An upper-class lady had four main duties: to obey her husband; to produce heirs to maintain the family line; to manage her household economy; to appear lady-like, through certain polite accomplishments.

- Ladies were expected to play an instrument such as the harpsichord, cultivate good tastes in decoration and master arts like embroidery, lace-making, drawing, singing, dancing and polite conversation.

- Many spent time paying and receiving social calls, shopping and doing charitable works among the poor.

- Sometimes, they helped with building projects on country houses, like Lady Dashwood at Kirtlington Park in the 1740s. Others held Court positions as ladies-in-waiting.

- Middling sort of women worked in workshops, taverns or in domestic service. They were expected to be money-earners, as well as having children and looking after their homes. Many worked alongside men.

- Poorer women took in spinning, laboured on farms or in industry, such as carrying baskets of coal up mineshafts. The growth of spinning mills widened work opportunities for women.

- These women, too, were expected to rear children, do domestic chores and manage a household.

- A few independent women grazed their own sheep, ran shops or taverns. Many were widows keeping businesses alive after a husband's death.

- Some women also became actresses, wet-nurses or fell into prostitution.

- The majority of women obediently did what was required of them, condemned to a second-class life with few legal rights.

(b) Explain the importance of women in this period. (10)

- Aristocrats, like Sarah Marlborough, worked hard behind the scenes and often influenced political decisions.

- Women were important elements in maintaining family dynasties through child-bearing and their part in arranged marriage settlements.

- Through running businesses and working, women contributed to the national economy and to Britain's long-term growth over the 1700s.

- Poorer women were often seen among rioters, especially protests directed against price rises. They thus demonstrated a show of political awareness, acting as a barometer by which the authorities could assess the impact of their policies.

- Women were important as consumers, stimulating the production of many fashionable goods to satisfy demand.

2. (a) Describe the main details of the rise of Louis XIV's power in Europe between about 1660 and 1702. (20)

- Louis XIV's aim, after 1661, was to establish France within her 'natural' frontiers; the sea, the Pyrenees, the Alps and the Rhine to the north. The problems lay in the north, with the Dutch.

- Louis attacked the Dutch (1667–1668), but was driven back. After the settlement at Aix-la-Chapelle, he was determined to continue his aggression.

- Another war against the Dutch followed (1672–1678). France, at the Treaty of Nymwegen, gained territory along its north-western border.

- In 1688, Louis attacked the Dutch again, as well as invading the Palatinate. England, the German Empire, Spain and Sweden formed the League of Augsburg and declared war against France.

- The Treaty of Ryswick (1697) resulted in only limited gains for Louis.

- By 1702, Louis wished to extend Bourbon power over Spain and her empire. The sick Charles II had no heir. Louis believed that he had a claim to the Spanish territories.

- After the failure of two Partition Treaties (1698 and 1700), Charles II made a will leaving his entire Spanish inheritance to Philip of Anjou, Louis' grandson.

- After Louis said that Anjou still retained a claim to the French throne, moved troops into the Spanish Netherlands and recognised James II's son as heir to the English crown, war became inevitable. The allies sought to preserve the European balance of power by preventing the union of France and Spain.

- England wished to maintain the Protestant succession.

(b) Explain how this affected the history of England at this time.　　　　(10)

- The threat of an increase in French power in Europe caused England to shift her diplomatic direction.

- During the early 1660s, England had been at war with the Dutch as commercial rivals. The Treaty of Breda (1667) led to an Anglo-Dutch alliance against Louis' threats. Louis' aggression strengthened this development until 1702, and beyond.

- William III's accession naturally united Anglo-Dutch interests against France.

- Louis' assaults on the Dutch were viewed as detrimental to England's European commercial interests.

- After 1701, with Louis' backing of the Old Pretender, a religious element crept in. England supported Protestants to restrict any increase of Catholic influence.

- The desire to limit French power, the realisation of the value of alliances for this and declarations of war, in 1689 and 1702, to maintain her interests, drew England closer into European affairs.

- Success in the Spanish Succession War established England as a great power during the 18th century.

3.　(a) Describe the main achievements of the architect, Christopher Wren.　　(20)

- Educated at Westminster School and Wadham College, Oxford, Wren studied anatomy, mathematics, physics and astronomy. He turned to architecture later in life.

- Wren was a skilled designer and model-maker, with a thorough understanding of the principles of Classical architecture.

- His chance to excel came when fire destroyed much of the City of London in 1666. He immediately produced a forward-looking plan for rebuilding the City.

- He was involved in creating the Monument to the Great Fire (1671–1676).

- Wren and his helpers designed over 50 new churches for London. Many had fine steeples, notable for their architectural variety. Some, like St Mary-le-Bow, still stand today.

- In 1673, Wren planned the rebuilding of St Paul's Cathedral. Construction began in 1675, the dome was complete by 1708, regular services started in 1716. Wren supervised all stages of the work and produced his masterpiece.

- Wren helped design a number of other buildings including the Royal Hospital, Greenwich, the Royal Observatory and alterations to St James's Palace.

- His works outside London included the Sheldonian Theatre, Tom Tower at Christ Church, Oxford, Trinity College Library, Cambridge and a royal palace at Winchester.

- His output of buildings was larger than any other English architect of his time.

- Wren established the architectural taste for Baroque Classicism in England which lasted for over 40 years. He is noted for the variety of his designs and for his ability to place Classical buildings on awkward Gothic foundations.

- Such was his fame, that other builders such as Christopher Kempster imitated him.

(b) Explain why you think it is important for historians to study the history of buildings and architectural design. (10)

- To learn about fashion and taste in the architectural style of a particular age and to study changes of style and design over time.

- To understand the construction of buildings; to examine building materials and their use.

- To look at the achievements of particular architects, artists and craftsmen, whether in stone, brick, wood, plaster, slate, iron or glass.

- To explore how building design followed function and contemporary practices, as in the layout of churches and the arrangement of rooms within country houses.

- To appreciate the differing domestic circumstances of all social ranks.

4. (a) Describe the career of Sir Isaac Newton. (20)

- Isaac Newton was born on Christmas Day 1642.

- He went up to Trinity College, Cambridge. Sent home during the plague year of 1665–1666, Newton is reputed to have studied the nature of light, the laws of gravity and differential calculus.

- In 1669, Newton became a professor of mathematics at Cambridge, dividing his time between mathematics, alchemy, astronomy and Bible study.

- In a paper of 1672, delivered to the Royal Society, Newton showed that white light consisted of a mixture of all colours. *Opticks*, his book on light, was published in 1704. It became the standard work for the next century.

- By 1684, Newton had formulated the Laws of Motion and the laws of gravitational forces.

- His great work, *Principia*, on the mathematical laws of mechanics and forces, appeared in 1687.

- Newton represented Cambridge University in Parliament in 1689 and again in 1701–1702. He became Warden of the Mint (1694), supervising recoinage, before promotion as Master in 1700. He presented coinage reports to the government in 1717–1718.

- A Fellow of the Royal Society since 1672, Newton was elected its President in 1703. He was re-elected annually until his death.

- Newton died in 1723. Such was his reputation that his body was laid in state and he was buried in Westminster Abbey. Many regarded him with awe as a symbol of the Enlightenment.

(b) Explain what you consider to be Newton's greatest achievement. (10)

- Arguably, Newton's greatest achievement was his *Principia* or *The Mathematical Principles of Natural Philosophy*. This book became a landmark in the history of science.

- Here, Newton set out the nature of space, time and motion; his laws of motion and his theories of gravity.

- Newton worked out new rules for reasoning which revolutionised scientific investigation. Through these, Newton went further than ever before in trying to answer unsolved scientific mysteries.

- This book not only advanced science, but validated much past scientific work. It also generated new analytical methods.

- *Principia* represented a breakthrough in the study of mathematics and physics. Its contents form the basis of much modern science and it is often regarded as the most influential scientific work up to the present time.

5. (a) Describe the main events of the Great Fire of London in 1666. (20)

- The fire began in the king's baker's shop in Pudding Lane, on Sunday, 2nd September 1666.

- Wooden houses, dry from the hot weather and packed closely together, enabled the blaze to spread quickly. The fire service was poor and, fanned by a strong easterly wind, flames engulfed the City.

- Blowing sparks spread the blaze. Pepys mentioned 'flakes of fire' and showers of 'firedrops', leaping from one house to another, and the intense heat which burnt the soles of people's feet.

- Evelyn described the panic and chaos as shrieking men, women and children hurried to save their goods as best they could in carts and boats.

- The fire destroyed over 13,000 houses, about 88 churches, 52 Company Halls and the Royal Exchange. Old St Paul's was burnt, but only about four or five people were killed. About 80% of the City suffered.

- Social problems arose as people became homeless. Many moved to areas like Moorfields, camping out in tents.

- There was a shortage of food. The poor suffered as bread prices doubled. Merchants suffered as their warehouses were destroyed and businesses faltered.

- There were unforeseen advantages. The plague was cleared. The fire offered an opportunity to re-construct the City. Wren's master plan was not carried out, but he rebuilt St Paul's in a Classical style, along with over 50 City churches. Houses were made of brick and stone. Streets were widened.

- No one knows the real cause of the fire. Perhaps the baker, Thomas Farynor, neglected his oven and it was an accident.

- There was talk of Dutch and French plots and Robert Hubert, a mad Frenchman, was hanged for supposedly starting the blaze.

(b) Explain what was done to try to stop the blaze. (10)

- Many efforts were made to stop the fire.

- Men with chains of buckets passed water from the river. Such pumping engines as could be arranged were brought into use.

- Houses were either pulled down or blown up to create fire-breaks in an attempt to stem the blaze.

- The Duke of York took charge of the City, co-ordinating the fire-fighting after the mayor proved to be incompetent.

- Sailors were brought in to fight the blaze.

- By Thursday, 6th September the fire had died down and burnt itself out.

C. Britain 1750–circa 1900

War and Rebellion

1. (a) Describe the main events of the Seven Years' War. (20)

- After a 'diplomatic revolution' in Europe, France and Austria, with Sweden and Saxony threatened Frederick of Prussia. In 1756, Frederick invaded Saxony to defend himself. Britain agreed to help. Thus began the Seven Years' War (1756–1763).

- Minorca was lost in 1756 and Admiral Byng was shot for cowardice in the following year.

- In Germany, the Duke of Cumberland was defeated at Hastenbach.

- Cumberland was then forced to sign the Klosterseven Convention by which he had to disband his army. England feared a French invasion.

- In India, in the 'Black Hole of Calcutta', British prisoners were shut in a small room without enough air or water. Only 21 out of 146 survived.

- Montcalm, the French General, drove back the British in Canada, while the French defeated General Braddock in North America, at Fort Dusquene.

- Pitt the Elder then took over the management of the war. Pitt was a brilliant war leader. He won support through his speeches in the Commons.

- Pitt wanted to support Prussia in Europe, thus keeping the French busy, while he strengthened British power in India and Canada.

- In 1757, Robert Clive's victory at Plassey ensured that Bengal was controlled by the East India Company.

- In Canada, Wolfe captured Quebec in 1759. Unfortunately, this success cost him his life.

- In 1759, the French were beaten at Minden and Admiral Hawke smashed a French fleet in Quiberon Bay. 1759 was seen as Britain's 'annus mirabilis'.

- In 1761, the British took Pondicherry from the French. Although Pitt championed expansion of the war, George III and his ministers did not.

- They had decided it was time to make peace.

(b) Explain why the result of this war was of great benefit to England.   (10)

- By the Treaty of Paris (1763) England benefited greatly, acquiring Canada, much of India and Minorca.

- England gained politically as extra territories meant more power, prestige and military influence.

- The opportunity for England to increase trade and expand her commercial empire brought economic benefits.

- Colonies were a source of raw materials and they provided overseas markets for goods manufactured in England. This stimulated the growth of industry in England.

2.   (a) Describe the circumstances leading to the outbreak of the American War of Independence in 1776.   (20)

- British victory in the Seven Years' War (1756–1763) brought worries over financing colonial defence against the French and the native Indians.

- This led to a series of British measures to tax the American Colonies which, in turn, led to a storm of colonial protest.

- The Sugar Act (1764) regulated colonial trade. The colonists were unrepresented at Westminster, so why should they submit to British taxation? 'No taxation without representation!' became their cry.

- To raise further revenue, Britain passed the Stamp Act (1765). Such was the opposition that it was repealed in 1766. However, a Declaratory Act (1766) maintained the British right to tax the colonies. This raised further protests.

- In 1767, the Townshend Duties imposed on a range of colonial goods, again increased tensions.

- British troops fired on a colonial crowd in the so-called Boston Massacre (1770). Colonial opposition erupted and, in 1773, at the Boston Tea Party, over 300 chests of tea were thrown into Boston Harbour in protest against import duties.

- In retaliation, the British government passed the Intolerable Acts (1774). Boston Harbour was closed until compensation was received for the destroyed tea; the Massachusetts Charter was cancelled and British troops were billeted in Boston homes.

- An American Continental Congress (1774) demanded a trade embargo on Britain and the withholding of taxes, by force if necessary. A second Congress (1775) voted to raise a colonial army.

- Words became shots at Lexington in 1775 as war approached. The Declaration of American Independence followed on 4 July 1776.

(b) Explain how the results of this war affected England's position in the world. (10)

- There was a temporary short-term decline in England's political reputation as a world power, but economic recovery was fast.

- After 1783 England co-operated with America favouring the internal development of its mainland to open up new markets and trade patterns for mutual advantage.

- While retaining American interests, England focused her energies on developing colonial interests in India, Australia and New Zealand.

- England's position grew increasingly global, embracing both the east and the west. She did not turn away from her former American colonies.

- The war made England look to her European position and be cautious. France, Spain and even Holland had sided with her enemy.

3. (a) Describe the major causes of the French Revolution in 1789. (20)

- Philosophers published new ideas generating a long-term cultural background of change.

- Montesquieu attacked Church privileges; Voltaire criticised French absolutism; Rousseau argued that Man was born free, but was everywhere in chains.

- Such thinkers supported the cause of Liberty and Equality against the long-established authority of Church, state and nobility.

- The Enlightenment spread notions of progress and of society perfecting itself through the development of freedom and equality.

- Louis XVI and Marie Antoinette were despised, seen as awkward, lazy, absolutist rulers, out of touch with their people.

- By 1789, the French government was corrupt, inefficient and bankrupt.

- Peasants hated the clergy and the nobility, who, through their high offices and estates, were rich but did not pay taxes.

- Peasants were controlled by a semi-feudal system. They were poor, starving and burdened with heavy dues like the salt tax and forced labour on roads.

- Craftsmen in towns were hampered by a rigid guild organisation.

- Short-term causes included a series of poor harvests, as in 1788. Famine led to civil unrest, especially in Paris.

- After the States General failed to act, the Third Estate broke away, called itself a National Assembly and swore an oath not to disband until the Constitution was reformed. Spontaneous anarchy followed with the storming of the Bastille on 14 July 1789. Revolution had begun.

(b) Explain why the French revolutionaries were able to chop off Louis XVI's head in 1793. (10)

- Louis XVI had shown himself to be untrustworthy when he tried to flee from Paris in July 1791.

- Owing to his stubborn attitude and his belief in Divine Right, Louis failed to compromise with the National Assembly or with any revolutionary leader.

- Any who might have saved Louis were either dead or exiled. He faced only his enemies.

- Louis was tried for treason, accused of plotting with counter-revolutionaries against his own people.

- No foreign rulers had been able effectively to come to Louis's aid.

- Revolutionaries wanted the king dead. In 1792, with the proclamation of the Republic, where there was no place for a king, Robespierre declared that Louis must die so that the state should live.

4. (a) Describe the main details of the Battle of Trafalgar. (20)

- On 21st October 1801, Nelson, with 27 British ships, engaged Villeneuve's Franco-Spanish fleet of 34 vessels, off Cape Trafalgar.

- Nelson's plan was to approach the enemy, break their line in half, surround that half and force a fight to the end.

- By 11.00 a.m., Nelson's fleet sailed in two parallel lines led by himself and Collingwood. Nelson was outnumbered and outgunned: 30,000 men and 2,500 guns against 17,000 men and 2,148 guns.

- At 11.45 a.m., Nelson signalled: 'England expects that every man will do his duty'.

- The Franco-Spanish ships were arranged in an uneven half-moon shape. Nelson attacked and split their line. The front ten enemy ships took no real part in the action.

- There followed a bloody battle as more English vessels crossed the line. It was a mêlée: some ships were locked together with individual ship-to-ship fighting at close quarters; there were broadsides and musketry. The British focused on damaging the hulls of the enemy ships.

- *Victory* locked masts with *Redoubtable* and Nelson was picked off by a sniper on her mizzen mast, as he directed operations from his quarter-deck. He was carried below and later died.

- The enemy fleet was gradually overwhelmed as more British ships entered the battle.

- The Franco-Spanish fleet was defeated. The front enemy ships sailed away. Britain captured 22 ships. The enemy lost 5,800 killed or wounded, against British casualties of 1,700 men.

(b) Explain what effect Nelson's victory had on the future conduct of the war against France. (10)

- Trafalgar was a decisive victory. The French lost so many ships that any threat of a French invasion of Britain was removed.

- Success at Trafalgar confirmed England's command of the sea and strengthened her military confidence.

- To break the deadlock between Britain and France, new ways had to be found of fighting the enemy indirectly. This resulted in the development of economic warfare. Napoleon issued the Berlin and Milan Decrees (1806 and 1807). This created the Continental System, banning France or ports under French control from trading with Britain. Britain retaliated, forbidding trade with France.

- Napoleon threatened England by building alliances against her, as in the Treaty of Tilsit with Russia (1807).

- Britain and her allies made a series of further coalitions until Napoleon was finally defeated at Waterloo in 1815.

5. (a) Describe the main events of the Crimean War (1854–1856). (20)

- In 1854, Britain and France supported Turkey against Russia. Russia was seen as dangerous, threatening Turkey and seeking to extend her power into the Black Sea, the Dardanelles and the Mediterranean.

- Lord Raglan was Commander-in-Chief of the British army. Troops were shipped to Balaclava, on the Crimean peninsula.

- The main war aims were to protect Constantinople, capture the Russian naval base of Sebastopol and, ultimately, defeat Russia.

- In September 1854, French and British armies landed to the north of Sebastopol and beat the Russians at the Battle of Alma. The Russians strengthened Sebastopol's defences. The allies besieged the port.

- In October 1854, the Russians attacked the British to save their fortress. The British defeated them at Balaclava, at which the Charge of the Light Brigade took place.

- The Russians were then beaten at the Battle of Inkerman in November 1854, again trying to break the allied siege of Sebastopol.

- Winter came on. The allied troops were still in summer uniforms. Supplies and medical arrangements were poor. Many soldiers died of disease.

- Florence Nightingale set up her hospital at Scutari and improved the level of medical care.

- In September 1855, the Malakov, the main defence in front of Sebastopol, was captured. The Russians then evacuated the fortress.

● Tsar Nicholas I died. His successor, Alexander II, was keen to make peace with Britain. This came through the Treaty of Paris (1856).

(b) Explain why England's leaders considered that it was important to enter this war. (10)

● England's leaders saw Russia as a threat to her imperial interests. Russia was a danger to India and England did not want any increase of Russian power in the Mediterranean.

● Russia had been trying to make deals with Turkey to gain access to the Mediterranean. It was British policy to support Turkey against the Russian menace. Britain feared Russian expansion into Europe at Turkish expense.

● England acted also to protect her economic and trading interests. She did not want any Russian competition either in the Mediterranean or the Baltic.

● Even though Turkey was supported, British politicians acted really only for British self-interest and self-preservation.

● England wished to maintain the current balance of power in Europe. She resented Russian attempts to 'rock the boat'.

6. (a) Describe the key events of the Indian Mutiny of 1857. (20)

● In May 1857, Sepoys at Meerut and Delhi mutinied against their British officers. Sepoy regiments in the north-west province followed suit.

● English settlements at Lucknow and Cawnpore were put under siege.

● There was bloodshed and horror on both sides. In Delhi, after recapturing the city, the British massacred the local population. At Cawnpore, Nana Sahib, on receiving the British surrender, massacred the men and over 200 women and children. After recapture by the British, Indian rebels were made to lick two square inches of floor clean of blood, before being hanged.

● Sepoys were blown from the mouths of cannons after the siege of Lucknow was relieved by Sir Henry Havelock.

● Indians saw the revolt as a national revolt against British rule, and had it spread as intended, the British position would have been weak. There were only about 40,000 European troops in India.

● In military terms, the Mutiny was a small-scale affair. Only in the Bengal army were there revolts and no more than 25% of Sepoys took part.

● Many areas remained neutral. The mutiny was never a war of independence. The revolt affected scarcely one third of British India; no foreign power intervened; there was little organised leadership; civil administration remained undisturbed in mutiny-free areas; frontiers were unaffected and the affair was crushed within five months.

(b) Explain why the mutiny broke out. (10)

● In the short term, the mutiny was caused by rumours that Lee-Enfield rifle cartridges were greased with pig and cow fat. As the end of the cartridge had to be bitten off, this offended both Muslims and Hindus.

- British power in India was expanding. In the 1830s, Lord Bentinck's policies of westernisation upset the Indians.

- Lord Dalhousie continued this trend believing that western technology meant progress. He built railways, telegraph systems and schools. Indians saw traditional values and culture disappearing.

- Ruthless British territorial expansion after 1848, through the Doctrine of Lapse, led to further Anglo-Indian tensions.

- The Indian cotton industry was weakened by cheap imports from Britain.

- Sepoys resented service in Burma.

- British officers tried to convert Indian troops to Christianity.

- Defeats in Afghanistan and setbacks in the Crimea destroyed the myth of British invincibility.

7. (a) Describe the main events of the Boer War (1899–1902). (20)

- After decades of tension between Britain and the Boers of the Transvaal and the Orange Free State, war came in 1899.

- Kruger, as leader of an independent Transvaal, wished to extend northwards; he taxed the Uitlanders; he wanted the British out and enlisted German support. This alarmed Britain.

- There was a British trade war with the Transvaal after 1894.

- Kruger reasserted Transvaal independence after the abortive Jameson Raid in 1895. This fuelled tensions. Again, Kruger received German support.

- Britain moved troops to the Transvaal borders, prompting a Boer ultimatum demanding their withdrawal. This was virtually a declaration of war.

- War came in 1899. The Boers, supplied with German weapons, believed that with 60,000 men, compared to the 14,000 British troops in South Africa, a quick victory would be theirs.

- The conflict was fierce and bloody, the Boers using guerrilla tactics well suited to their terrain.

- In 1899, the Boers seized Kimberley, Mafeking and Ladysmith, and defeated the British at Stormberg, Magersfontein and the Tugela River.

- However, 250,000 fresh British troops arrived under Lord Roberts. They wore down the Boers under Cronje.

- In 1900, the Orange Free State was knocked out when Bloemfontein was captured. Ladysmith and Mafeking were relieved. The British occupied Johannesburg and Pretoria. Kruger fled to Holland.

- Commando units under Botha, de Wet and Smuts continued fighting until 1902, but the Boers were defeated.

- Kitchener was harsh on the Boers. Concentration camps were set up for prisoners, including women and children. Many died of hardship or disease.

(b) Explain the consequences of this war for Britain. (10)

- The Transvaal and the Orange Free State lost their independence, becoming British colonies by the Treaty of Vereeniging (1902).

- Britain promised them self-government. They received separate parliaments in 1906.

- In 1910, the Union of South Africa was established with one parliament at Cape Town. The functioning of the Union benefited Britain, with relative peace and the hope of trade profits.

- The part played in the Union by former enemies, such as Botha, suggested that Britain had achieved some success in South Africa.

- Britain gained a political and military ally in South Africa.

- Despite victory, opposition grew to the manner of her imperial conduct, and Britain ceased her policies of aggressive colonial conquest.

8. (a) Describe the career of the Duke of Wellington in the war against France. (20)

- Wellington fought against the French in many places. In 1794, he took part in the Flanders campaign in the French Revolutionary Wars.

- In 1796, he was sent to India, establishing a fine military reputation with victories (1803) at Assaye and Argaum over the Mahrattas.

- Arriving in Portugal in 1808, Wellington played a major part in the Peninsular War. He won the Battle of Vimeiro, after which he faced a court enquiry for signing the truce of Cintra, granting easy terms to the defeated French.

- After Sir John Moore's death (1809), Wellington assumed command of the British army in the Peninsular. He was determined to defeat the French.

- Wellington showed his all-round genius as a commander. As a defensive measure, in 1809, he constructed the Lines of the Torres Vedras to prevent the British Army from being driven into the sea.

- He was brave in attack, as in the assaults at Badajoz and Ciudad Rodrigo (1812). At Salamanca (1812), he destroyed the main French field army in Spain. His victory at Vitoria (1813) ended Napoleon's Spanish rule. The French retreated over the Pyrenees.

- By 1813, Wellington was respected in Europe as the most famous British General since Marlborough.

- Commanding the British Army at Waterloo in 1815, Wellington, with the help of Blücher and the Prussians, put an end to Napoleon's hope of a return to power.

- Throughout his military career, Wellington had been the scourge of the French.

(b) Explain the importance of what you consider to be his most famous victory. (10)

- It may be argued that Wellington's defeat of Napoleon at Waterloo on 18 June 1815 ranks as his most famous victory.

- In military terms, this represented a major French disaster. They were soundly beaten, suffering 25,000 killed or wounded and losing 9,000 as prisoners. Even the Imperial Guard were overcome.

- The battle marked the end of the French Revolutionary and Napoleonic Wars.

- Waterloo confirmed Wellington's fame and greatness as a military commander.

- Politically, Waterloo meant the end of Napoleon and his dream of European domination. It also helped the restoration of the French monarchy.

Government and Parliament

1. (a) Describe the main details of the 1832 Reform Bill. (20)

- In June 1832, the First Reform Bill passed through Parliament after several setbacks. In the end, Wellington and many of the Tory opponents of the Bill stayed away from the Lords so that Grey could achieve his political success.

- In boroughs, the franchise was given to those householders worth more than £10 per year.

- In the countryside, the vote went to 40/- freeholders, £10 copyholders and tenants-at-will with land worth more than £50 a year.

- Boroughs with a population of less than 2,000 people lost both MPs. Those with between 2,000 and 4,000 inhabitants lost one of their members.

- 143 seats were redistributed among the growing new towns, such as Manchester and Sheffield.

- Owing to these changes, about one sixth of the male population gained the vote.

- Although industrial interests were more represented, landowners remained strong. For example, in the Parliament of 1841–1846, 70% of MPs came from the landed classes.

- The Bill did not introduce a secret ballot and the working classes were still excluded from the franchise.

- The political reform of 1832 favoured the middle class and the Bill was not as far-reaching as some reformers had wished.

(b) Explain why this act was thought to be necessary. (10)

- The pre-1832 system was outdated. Inequality of parliamentary representation meant that new cities like Leeds and Birmingham had no MPs.

- Rotten boroughs, often deserted places, such as Old Sarum, enjoyed full parliamentary representation.

- Pocket boroughs, controlled by wealthy patrons to secure government majorities, added to the unfairness.

- Elections were corrupt with no secret ballot. There was variation in those eligible to vote. The system failed to handle the growth of the population and the expansion of industrial centres.

- An emerging middle class provided a momentum for parliamentary reform.

- Radical leaders, like William Cobbett and Henry Hunt, demanded a widening of political representation. Groups such as the National Union of the Working Class, founded in 1830, demanded political change.

- Revolutions abroad, like that in France in 1830, fired the wish for constitutional development.

- Riots in London, Bristol and Derby provided the ghost of revolution from below, encouraging some MPs to advocate reform from above before it became too late.

2. (a) Describe the most important political beliefs of the Chartists. (20)

- The Chartists, led by William Lovett, were a group of working-class reformers seeking the vote for all men.

- In 1836, the London Working Men's Association set out six demands. Their ideal was to form a democracy to attain political power as the first stage of a new economic order in society.

- The Chartists demanded: universal male suffrage; equal electoral districts; annual Parliaments; the payment of MPs; a secret ballot and the end of the property qualification for MPs.

- William Lovett named these six points 'The People's Charter'. Support grew and the movement spread to Birmingham by 1838.

- Many rank-and-file Chartists, not understanding the high ideals of the Charter, were more concerned with their local grievances.

- Lovett's initial wish was to draw the working class together, using every legal method to give all ranks of society equal political rights.

- Chartism became weakened through disagreements over how their ideals should be attained. Lovett and Thomas Attwood believed in peaceful persuasion to achieve their wishes.

- Fergus O'Connor, through his newspaper *The Northern Star*, advocated force and violence. Along with George Harney, O'Connor won great support among the northern industrial towns.

- These differences within Chartism weakened the movement.

(b) Explain how far you think that the Chartists were successful in achieving their aims. (10)

- In the short term, the Chartists failed. Their petitions to Parliament in 1839, 1842 and 1848 were heavily rejected by a House of Commons dominated by the landed class.

- Riots, such as those in Newport in 1839 were crushed and increased suspicion of the movement.

- Economic recovery during the 1840s weakened Chartism, and Chartist opposition to the Anti-Corn Law League cut them off from a successful reforming group whose aims also favoured the working class.

- On the other hand, Chartism made some of the upper classes reconsider their views and sympathy for reform grew.

- Political rights for the working class, although largely achieved through the Reform Bills of 1867 and 1884, owed something to the influence of Chartism.

- Chartist ideals of a secret ballot and payment of MPs were achieved in 1872 and 1911, respectively. Of the Charter's six points, five are now practised. Annual Parliaments would be impractical!

- Thus, in the long term, the Chartists were successful.

3. (a) Describe the career of the political thinker, Jeremy Bentham. (20)

- Bentham was born in 1748. Educated at Westminster School and Oxford, he qualified as a barrister, although never practised. Instead, he became a political thinker.

- In 1776, he published *A Fragment of Government*, in which he argued that British government practice could be improved.

- His major work, *Introduction to the Principles of Morals and Legislation*, appeared in 1789. Here, Bentham put forward his theories of Utilitarianism.

- By this, all laws and government policies should lead to the greatest happiness of the greatest number. Institutions should be tested by one simple question. What is their utility or usefulness? If they failed to justify themselves, they should be swept away.

- Happiness was thought of as meaning peace, good law and public order.

- Bentham's ideas challenged traditional class privileges and vested interests, both in government and law.

- His book, *The Rationale of Punishments and Rewards*, attacked the harsh punishments of the Penal System.

- Bentham gained international recognition for his work. In 1792, he was made a French citizen. He was honoured also by Russia and America.

- In 1817, he attacked the electoral system, demanding annual Parliaments, a secret ballot and the vote for all men over the age of 21.

- Bentham criticised the Poor Law, making suggestions later accepted by Whig reformers.

- He died in 1832, on the day before the passing of the Great Reform Bill.

(b) Explain Bentham's importance as a political reformer. (10)

- Bentham had a great influence on the parliamentary reform movement of 1815–1832 and the Whig reforms of 1831–1841.

- Much of his thinking lay behind the legal, social, economic and political reforms of the whole 19th century.

- Bentham played an important role in changing society as an international political thinker.

- He was not a violent revolutionary as he desired progress through Parliament. Thus, his work served to reinforce the need to change the Constitution as the composition of society altered.

- Bentham provided inspiration to the agents of reform.

- Bentham's philosophy was spread through *The Westminster Review*. He also supported the founding of University College, London, set up, in part, to introduce new ideas to society's future leaders.

4. (a) Describe the main events of Robert Peel's career as Prime Minister 1841–1846.   (20)

- Robert Peel had a modern outlook, seeing the need for reform.

- He wished to make Britain a cheap place for living and supported the idea of free trade to reduce living costs and to stimulate trade.

- His Budgets of 1842, 1844, 1845 and 1846, abolished many export and import duties. By 1846, over 75% of duties existing in 1841 had been scrapped.

- Peel stabilised the currency by the Bank Charter Act (1844).

- He introduced income tax at 7d in the pound on incomes over £150 a year, hitting the upper and middle classes. His financial policies were successful. By 1844, government income exceeded spending by £2 million.

- Peel supported Shaftesbury in social reforms. The Mines Act (1842) introduced limited inspections and forbade women and girls, and boys under ten to work underground.

- His factory Act of 1844 improved conditions by limiting the number of daily workable hours. Many such reforms were opposed by Whigs and Tories alike, arguing that they would lead to a loss of profits and output. Government interference was also resented.

- In 1841, Daniel O'Connell demanded the repeal of the Anglo-Irish Union. Peel set up a Commission (1843) to examine the land problem, but the essential difficulties in Ireland remained.

- In June 1846, Peel allowed the repeal of the Corn Laws. Duties on wheat, barley and oats were abolished.

- Repeal of the Corn Laws, and the defeat of a Coercion Bill for Ireland, increased opposition to Peel. In 1846, he was forced to resign.

(b) Explain what you consider to have been his greatest political achievement.   (10)

- Even though it contributed to his downfall, the Repeal of the Corn Laws might be regarded as Peel's greatest political achievement.

- Through the Repeal, Peel increased England's trade. Other countries eased duties on English goods owing to the lifting of restrictions on corn imports.

- The Repeal was popular with reformers. Peel caught the mood of the time, offering reform at home when there was revolution abroad.

- The Repeal ensured that change in Britain occurred by evolution rather than revolution, by strengthening the idea that Parliament had sacrificed the Corn Laws to feed its people.

- The notion of Repeal suited Peel's sympathies for freer trade. He put principle before popularity in the economic interests of his country.

Religion and Social Reform

1. (a) Describe the development of Methodism and its main features in this period. (20)

- Methodism originated at Oxford with John and Charles Wesley in the 1730s and, influenced by George Whitefield and others, developed throughout the next two centuries.

- In 1784, John Wesley established an annual Methodist Conference as the movement expanded. At this stage, it was still part of the Anglican Church. The break came in 1795, when the Methodist Conference agreed to administer Anglican Sacraments.

- Methodism grew through breakaway groups, such as Independent Methodists (1805), Primitive Methodists (1810) and Wesleyan Reformers (1849). By 1850, the Methodist Church numbered about 500,000 people. These groups were characterised more by differences of organisation rather than doctrine. Most were reunited by 1932.

- There were different developments in Wales with much field-preaching and eventual separation from the Anglicans in 1811. Throughout the 1800s, Wales was largely non-conformist.

- In doctrine, Methodists stressed personal salvation through faith and an evangelical enthusiasm. Open-air preaching was commonplace and lay-preachers toured the country. Methodists encouraged Bible study and hymns, many originally written by Charles Wesley.

- Temperance, thrift and hard work were features of the religion. These virtues brought rewards and some Wesleyan chapels in the north of England were dominated by rich mill-owners.

- Methodism, though, generally appealed to working-class groups, such as miners, neglected by the Church of England.

(b) Explain how successful the Methodist movement had become by 1900. (10)

- By 1900, Methodism was successful, having a wide influence over all society, especially the working classes.

- Success came through its careful organisation with the establishment of preaching circuits based on chapels. Most towns and villages had their Methodist chapel with its social and religious network of care and concern for the welfare of members.

- Methodism provided many opportunities for active participation in spreading the Faith through lay-preaching, Sunday-school teaching or leading prayer-groups.

- Methodism flourished through its involvement in movements such as Chartism and Trade Unionism.

- Its beliefs could easily transform the life of any servant, miner or farm labourer who 'found Jesus'. As such, it gave hope to all people, however humble, suggesting that there was a place for them in God's world.

- Methodism prospered because it was easily accessible to all.

2. (a) Describe the main details of the Roman Catholic Emancipation Act of 1829. (20)

- The Roman Catholic Emancipation Act led to the achievement of full civil rights for Roman Catholics. It was passed against strong opposition from George IV.

- The 1829 Act allowed Catholics to play a full part in political life.

- The Test Act and the Corporation Act, which had restricted Catholic political rights by preventing them from holding the most important state offices, or from being members of town corporations, were abolished.

- Roman Catholics, except for priests, were permitted to sit in Parliament as MPs.

- Catholic monks and nuns were banned, but this order was not carried out.

- Most major state positions were opened to Catholics, apart from the offices of Lord Chancellor, Keeper of the Great Seal and Lord Lieutenant of Ireland.

- The practice of Roman Catholicism was permitted, but priests were not allowed to wear clerical dress outside their churches.

- The Emancipation Act destroyed the notion that Britain was entirely a Protestant country, although the 1701 Act of Settlement, banning a Catholic monarch, remained in force.

- The special union between Church and state, created in 1689, was shattered by the Act.

(b) Explain how this Act came into being and why it was considered necessary. (10)

- Roman Catholics did not have full rights. For example, no Catholic could be elected to Parliament.

- By 1829, there were many political and economic problems in Ireland, where 80% of the population was Catholic, yet Catholics had no parliamentary means of sorting out their grievances.

- Irish protests were led by Daniel O'Connell. He demanded the repeal of the Act of Union (1801) and an independent Irish Parliament for the conduct of home affairs. Catholic Emancipation was necessary for this.

- Protests by the Roman Catholic Association and by Catholic clergy led to a strong Irish movement for emancipation.

- The election of O'Connell for County Clare in 1828 raised the possibility of civil war in Ireland.

- This pressure forced Wellington to reverse his anti-Emancipation position and to work with Peel to pass the Act.

3. (a) Describe the work of Elizabeth Fry as a prison reformer. (20)

- Elizabeth Fry, a quaker from a rich banking family, was determined to improve conditions in prisons, particularly for women and children.

- After a visit to Newgate Prison in 1813, she was horrified by the squalid conditions in which female prisoners and children lived. She publicised her findings, resulting in Newgate being declared a public nuisance in 1814.

- Elizabeth continued to work tirelessly for prison reform until her death in 1845. In 1817, she founded an association to improve living standards in prisons. In the following year, she publicised poor prison conditions when giving evidence to a parliamentary commission.

- She travelled widely, both in England and in Europe, and pressurised governments to improve their prisons. She even attracted royal patronage.

- Elizabeth visited prisoners. She tried to help them by teaching them the basic principles of Christianity. She insisted on providing useful work for prison inmates. She tried to improve the quality of prison food.

- She was also concerned with the wretched conditions of women convicts transported to Australia. Between 1818 and 1843, it was said that Elizabeth visited over 100 convict ships.

- She spread her ideas through her strength of mind and personality and encouraged others to follow her example. By such means, she widened her circle of supporters and thus fostered the movement for prison reform.

(b) Explain the reasons for the beginning of the movement to reform prisons. (10)

- Prisons were badly run. They were dirty, violent, overcrowded and centres of vice and crime.

- The poor conditions in prisons attracted people desiring reform. Men like John Howard first brought the miseries of prison inmates to public notice. This was then taken up by other individuals such as Elizabeth Fry.

- Interest in prison reform grew and was finally pursued by MPs like Romilly, Burdett and Lord Holland.

- This, in turn, resulted in a parliamentary commission to investigate the conditions in London prisons with a view to improving them.

- Once Parliament was involved and the reform movement had attracted some influential supporters, the idea of improvement became a reality.

Social and Economic History

1. (a) Describe the main developments of the Agricultural Revolution. (20)

- Since the Middle Ages most farming had been conducted following the old, inefficient three-field system. Crop yields were low. The population rose during the 18th century, so new ways of farming were needed. These new ways are called the Agricultural Revolution.

- Intensive enclosure of the landscape took place after about 1750. There had been enclosure before then, but the pace quickened. Enclosure was carried out by private Acts of Parliament. Over 4,000 Acts were passed between 1760 and 1800. In 1801, the General Enclosure Act made the process easier.

- New four-course rotations were introduced, with crops like turnips providing winter food for animals.

- A newer scientific approach developed. Selective breeding was introduced. Robert Bakewell produced his Dishley cattle and New Leicester sheep. These were larger, better quality animals, yielding more meat and milk. Better fertilisers, marls and manures became more widespread.

- New ploughs, horse-hoes, harrows and seed drills were developed. Later, came steam ploughing and threshing, using stationary engines in fields.

- Improvement was stimulated by aristocrats like Thomas Coke and Lord Townshend pioneering new methods on their estates. George III at Windsor also made new farming fashionable.

- Ideas were spread by a growing literature, such as the Board of Agriculture Reports detailing the latest practices.

- It has been argued that there was no true Agricultural Revolution. Developments were piecemeal, uneven across the country and the rate of change was slow. On the other hand, 1700–1850 saw agricultural output increase by 2½ to 3 times.

(b) Explain the good and bad effects of agricultural change on different groups of people within England. (10)

- Rich farmers and landowners sold more produce at higher prices.

- Through enclosure, they also consolidated their landholdings into more efficient agricultural units.

- Landowners profited from an increase in rents after enclosure. For instance, rents tripled on the Duke of Rutland's estates in the Vale of Belvoir.

- Poorer farmers suffered. Many could not afford the high costs of enclosure or of new machinery. Some lost status, becoming landless, agricultural labourers.

- Cottagers and squatters living on the commons lost their means of existence as wastes were enclosed.

- In some areas, the poor were driven from the countryside, seeking work in the developing urban factories.

2. (a) Describe the benefits of the development of railways during the Industrial Revolution. (20)

- Increased movement of goods stimulated the economy. There was better food distribution, such as fresh fish coming inland.

- The coal and iron industries profited. By 1850, locomotives were using over one million tons of coal annually.

- Railways provided new jobs. Over 300,000 navvies were employed by 1847. Engineering skills were required, as were people to run the system – over 60,000 by 1851.

- Geographical mobility increased. More people moved out of their towns or villages. Over half a million passengers travelled on the London to Birmingham line during its first year (1839).

- Travel gave people wider horizons and led to the growth of political ideas. In turn, this stimulated movements for reform.

- After 1844, there was cheap transport for the poor. Each railway company was required to provide at least one daily train, running at a rate of one penny per mile.

- Seaside towns like Blackpool, Scarborough and Brighton developed, along with the South Coast resorts. The annual summer holiday became a tradition.

- Derby, Crewe and Swindon expanded as new centres of railway building and engineering.

- Soccer developed as England's national game with the growth of the football leagues.

- Business practice itself evolved with more Joint Stock Companies. Financial investment in railways became an alternative to government stocks.

- Collectively, the nation benefited. Railway growth gave a practical demonstration of the idea of improvement, helping to make Britain 'the workshop of the world'.

(b) Explain why the revolution in steam transport did not help everyone in Britain.　　(10)

- Investors in turnpike trusts and new roads suffered as the railway network expanded carrying a greater volume of traffic at faster speeds.

- Long-distance stagecoach travel declined by the 1850s as road gave way to rail. There were fewer jobs in this service.

- The owners of large coaching inns also faced mounting losses as their businesses faltered.

- Canal owners and workers were displeased. Canal use declined. Although ideal for carrying heavy or fragile goods, water transport was too slow to compete with trains.

- Canal-company investors lost money as their shares fell in value. Shares in the Grand Junction Canal Company peaked at £330. They dropped to £155 in 1846 and were worth only £60 by 1853.

3.　(a) Describe the main developments in textile manufacturing during the Industrial Revolution.　　(20)

- A series of inventions in the textile industry transformed the old domestic system, with its small-scale cottage operations, into an organisation of large mills with new methods of mass production. This marked the start of Britain's Industrial Revolution.

- In 1733, John Kay invented the Flying Shuttle, a machine that wove broadcloth at great speed. This was still used in cottages.

- James Hargreaves' Spinning Jenny (1764) spun eight or more spindles on one treadle and increased the speed of spinning.

- Richard Arkwright, dreaming of large-scale production methods, produced his Water Frame (1769). This was too large for cottage use, so the first factory was set up at Cromford (Derbyshire) in 1771. Thus began the factory system.

- At first, machines were water-powered. Later, steam engines were used. Further technological developments followed, with Samuel Crompton's Spinning Mule (1779) and Edmund Cartwright's power loom (1785).

- A bleaching process followed by 1790. Thomas Bell developed fabric printing using a cylinder (1783). New, improved, power looms were manufactured by Radliffe and Horrocks after 1815.

- Samuel Greg started a factory at Styal in 1784. Other business kings emerged: Oldknow in Stockport, Horrocks in Preston and Peel in Bury.

- Large spinning mills grew up in towns like Manchester, Oldham, Bolton, Derby and Preston.

- Textile manufacturing boomed, accounting for 60% of Britain's exports during the 1850s.

(b) Explain why the Industrial Revolution first took place in Britain. (10)

- Britain had a good transport system. Roads, canals, railways and shipping developed between 1700 and 1850. Excellent ports grew up, such as London, Bristol, Liverpool and Hull. No internal customs barriers hampered the movement of goods.

- Technological innovation increased the speed and volume of manufacturing.

- Population growth generated an increasing domestic market for produce. British imperial expansion created overseas markets and established global trade patterns.

- A good labour supply existed. Domestic raw materials, like coal and iron ore, were plentiful. Foreign expansion gave access to raw materials from colonies, such as cotton from India.

- Efficient banking and credit systems enabled business enterprise to flourish, supported by an enlightened aristocracy, such as the Duke of Bridgewater pioneering canals or Lord Scarbrough developing coal mining in Yorkshire.

- Britain had an early lead and few rivals.

4. (a) Describe the most important achievements of Isambard Kingdom Brunel. (20)

- Brunel was an engineer and designer. After working with his father on the construction of a Thames tunnel, he began his own projects.

- Brunel was Chief Engineer to the Great Western Railway (1833–1846). He built the line from London to Bristol, surveying the whole route personally and favouring broad-gauge track of 7ft ¼in.

- This railway contained several feats of engineering and design, with great stations at the termini, Paddington (1854) and Bristol Temple Meads (1840), and smaller stations in an Italian style, such as at Charlbury.

- The line also featured a series of embankments and viaducts. Box tunnel, outside Bath, at 3,212 yards, ranks as one of Brunel's greatest achievements.

- Brunel engineered lines in the south-west of England, constructing, in all, over 1,000 miles of railway track.

- Brunel built ships. He had a vision of passengers travelling directly from London to New York, crossing the Atlantic from Bristol. His *Great Western* (1837) was constructed of wood. But *The Great Britain* (1843), made of metal, became the first iron-hulled, propeller-driven ship to cross the Atlantic. His epic ship, *The Great Eastern*, was a commercial flop.

- He designed and constructed bridges such as: the Albert Bridge (1855), over the Tamar, the Clifton Suspension Bridge (1864) at Bristol and the Maidenhead railway bridge over the Thames (1855).

- Brunel worked on docks, creating the Bristol Floating Harbour (1830–1831). He even improved heavy guns, some of which were used in the Crimean War.

- Brunel was an innovator, ever pushing forward with his experiments, such as those with propeller-driven ships and the use of gas for propulsion.

(b) Explain Brunel's importance to the industrial development of Britain. (10)

- Brunel developed a transport system helping industrial growth through the cheaper and faster movement of goods.

- He increased geographical mobility and his schemes for an Atlantic crossing began to open up the world.

- His achievements encouraged the expansion of activities such as engineering, building, technology, coal and iron.

- Brunel developed the idea of urban industrial specialisation, as when Swindon grew into a railway town.

- The whole industrial process was stimulated by the example of Brunel's achievements, his vision, his large-scale projects, his drive, determination and Victorian confidence.

5. (a) Describe the main stages in the development of the police force within this period. (20)

- Britain had no effective police force before the 19th century. Law and order were maintained through parish constables responsible to local Justices of the Peace.

- The Bow Street Runners, organised in London as thief-takers, by Henry Fielding, had received authority by 1757 to enforce order outside the city.

- In 1829, Robert Peel established the Metropolitan Police Force. These officers wore uniform. They carried a short baton and were strictly controlled from their headquarters at Scotland Yard. This arrangement of 'bobbies' or 'peelers' worked well and the police gradually became accepted.

- Boroughs were required to create similar forces under the Municipal Corporations Act (1835). In 1839, Justices of the Peace were meant to do likewise in their counties.

- Compulsory forces appeared under the County and Borough Police Act (1856), where county and borough constabularies were made responsible to the Home Office.

- By 1888, County Councils shared control of the police with Justices of the Peace.

- Working conditions and pay were standardised by the Police Act (1919), but Britain had no centralised police. Forces were locally regulated.

- Plain-clothes detectives came to London in 1842. The CID was finally set up in 1878. During the 1880s, a 'Special Branch' emerged to monitor particular threats to the government.

(b) Explain why it was important for Britain to improve its methods of enforcing law and order during the 19th century. (10)

- Population growth extended the volume and type of crime. There was a need to control increasing vice, gambling, theft and drink.

- The new middle classes were anxious during periods of crisis and repression, such as that c.1790–c.1821.

- The maintenance of public order became an issue especially during times of unrest, like reform and trade-union meetings and the strikes of the 1880s.

- New kinds of crowd emerged, often peaceful but still requiring control, such as those at football matches.

- The old system, based on the rural parish with constables and Justices of the Peace, was unsuitable for the new social situations in overcrowded, industrial, urban communities.

- As the size and structure of the population changed, so had the methods of policing it, in order to secure effective regulation.

- As central government increasingly regulated more aspects of life, it was expected that it would devise an effective, yet acceptable, organisation to contain crime and maintain good order.

6. (a) Describe the background to the trial of the Tolpuddle Martyrs in 1834. (20)

- In 1834, six farm labourers – George and James Loveless, John and Thomas Stanfield, James Brine and James Hammett – from Tolpuddle in Dorset, were prosecuted, accused of having administered illegal oaths for 'seditious' purposes. They had formed a trade union to agitate against low wages.

- Found guilty, they were sentenced to seven years' transportation. After a public outcry, they were pardoned in 1836.

- Unions had been legal since 1824, but governments were alarmed by them, in particular their use of secret rituals.

- After 1815, there was crisis. Luddites smashed machines; post-war unemployment was high; famine raged in 1816; corn remained expensive owing to the Corn Laws; rural and urban unrest were commonplace.

- The 1832 Reform Bill did nothing for the working classes.

- Workers began banding together in unions to improve pay and conditions – a movement inspired by Robert Owen.

- By 1832, cotton spinners had a union. The Operative Builders Union numbered over 60,000. Owen's Grand National Consolidated Trade Union had 500,000 members by 1834.

- Union activity generated government panic. Repression followed. Members were arrested. Agrarian unrest during the 1830s resulted in nine hangings, 400 men imprisoned and over 450 transportations.

- The Tolpuddle case occurred against a background of social and political unrest coupled with government fear. Their harsh punishment was no surprise.

(b) Explain the importance of the Tolpuddle case for the working-class movement of the time. (10)

- The Tolpuddle case suggested that the Whig governments were against the working classes, showing neither sympathy nor understanding of the working-class movement.

- The heavy sentence showed the high level of government fear.

- The eventual pardon, the initial outcry over their sentence and the parliamentary petition on their behalf, demonstrated the extent of working-class support for the cause of reform during the 1830s.

- The Martyrs' harsh punishment hardened working-class opposition to government, strengthening their determination to press ahead with the cause of trade-union reform and expansion.

- Subsequent improvement in working-class conditions, through further Reform Bills and the development of trade unions, resulted in part from the Tolpuddle Martyrs.

7. (a) Describe the most important events in the development of trade unions up to 1901. (20)

- Trade unions grew out of combinations of workers uniting to improve pay and conditions. Banned by the Combination Acts of 1799–1800, unions were legal by 1824.

- Thereafter, union growth was local and piecemeal. By 1832, the Union of Operative Builders numbered 60,000.

- In 1834, Robert Owen founded his Grand National Consolidated Union in an effort to form a general union for every trade. Despite its membership of over 500,000, this project collapsed.

- Government opposition, shown by the Tolpuddle case (1834), failed to dampen union expansion. The movement was further stimulated by the Chartists (1836–1848).

- In 1851, the Amalgamated Society of Engineers emerged as the first national union of skilled workers.

- A legal ruling against the Boilermakers' Union (1867) that its funds were unprotected by law, led to demands for full legal recognition of unions.

- In 1868, the Trade Union Congress was formed from councils of skilled workers. These had played an important role in securing limited working-class rights in the 1867 Reform Bill.

- After violent action by trade unionists in Sheffield, a government commission examined the whole union question.

- The Trade Union Act and the Criminal Law Amendment Act (1871) recognised the legality of union property, but declared strikes illegal.

- The Conspiracy and Protection of Property Act strengthened unions by giving them the right to strike.

- By 1888, union membership stood at about 750,000, rising to over 4 million by 1901 as more semi-skilled and unskilled workers became organised.

- The Taff Vale Case (1901), with a court ruling that unions were liable for damage done to an employer, weakened the powerful strike weapon and represented a blow to union power.

(b) Explain how trade unions tried to improve workers' lives. (10)

- Initially, unions strove for legal existence in order to improve workers' lives.

- They pressed for shorter working hours, better conditions and more pay.

- They wanted death, sickness or unemployment benefits for their members.

- Unions used a variety of methods in an effort to achieve their aims. These included strikes, negotiation and collective bargaining with employers.

- Their political agenda involved support for radical reformers, petitions to Parliament and championing parliamentary reform.

General Topics

1. (a) Describe what was on offer for visitors to see at the Great Exhibition of 1851. (20)

- The Great Exhibition, held in Crystal Palace, an iron and glass structure built in Hyde Park by Joseph Paxton, featured over 100,000 exhibits from all over the world. It was an international trade show of the works of industry of all nations.

- Half was devoted to British goods, divided into sections: raw materials, machinery, inventions, manufactures and sculpture.

- Items featured included printing presses, pumps, railway locomotives, carriages, steam hammers, machine tools, giant lathes and working power looms.

- Further exhibits comprised: agricultural machinery, Sheffield cutlery, a range of Yorkshire woollens and Birmingham products like locks, wrought-ironwork, buttons, guns and springs.

- There were English minerals, iron-framed pianos and even a chair carved from coal.

- On view were silks, lace, embroidery, clocks, military items, naval architecture, model ships, anatomical models, glass chandeliers, a range of toys and wax flowers.

- New inventions included a display of gas-lighting systems.

- From further afield came French tapestries, china and bronze; Belgian and Austrian furniture; Russian vases, ornaments, cloths, timber and furs; American farming machinery and raw materials.

- Featured, too, was a variety of products from places as diverse as Persia, Greece, Italy, Egypt, Turkey, Spain, Portugal, Sweden and Denmark.

- There were sculptures, full-size trees, a huge fountain and a range of exotic, tropical plants.

(b) Explain the importance of the Exhibition for Britain. (10)

- The Exhibition demonstrated the speed of Britain's technological progress. Queen Victoria commented that machines now did 'in a few instants' what used to take months.

- British achievements were celebrated. Britain was shown off as the most advanced industrial nation on the planet – the workshop of the World, with an endless variety of business enterprise.

- The nation was put on display. Its wealth and economic power were made apparent, elements which had political and military implications in world politics.

- The size and diversity of Britain's growing empire was reflected through the range of raw materials and manufactured goods.

- It was also meant to attract new business customers and stimulate further trade.

- The Great Exhibition portrayed the British sense of solidarity, confidence and Victorian optimism. It put the 'great' into Great Britain.

2. (a) Describe the main stages of the development of the British Empire in this period. (20)

- The British Empire grew steadily. Reasons included wars of conquest, treaty gains, trading-company expansion, exploration, colonisation, settlement of new territories and emigration.

- In the 1880s, apologists, like Rhodes, fostered a mood of 'aggressive imperialism'.

- By 1750, England's empire was largely commercial with interests in her north-American colonies, several Caribbean islands, Gibraltar and trading posts in India, such as Madras and Calcutta.

- Acquisition of Indian lands continued through the Treaty of Paris (1763) and policies like the Doctrine of Lapse after 1848. Oudh was annexed in 1856. India eventually became Britain's 'jewel in the crown' of the Empire.

- Canada was acquired in 1763. The loss of the American Colonies (1783) represented only a temporary set-back for British imperialism. Developments occurred elsewhere. Captain Cook explored Australia and New Zealand in the 1770s, leading to the establishment of British power.

- Britain gained the Cape Colony in 1815. In 'the scramble for Africa', she soon controlled Ghana, the Gold Coast and most of the southern and eastern areas of the continent.

- Interests grew in the Far East. After the Opium Wars with China, Britain gained Hong Kong by the Treaty of Nanking (1842).

- Other gains included Cylon (1802) and Cyprus (1878). Involvement was maintained in the Middle East. Egypt, although never a true colony, was monitored closely owing to British interests in the Suez Canal.

- By 1901, the Empire was huge, with an estimated population of over 398 million people. It was claimed that 'the sun never set' on British possessions.

(b) Explain the ways in which Britain benefited from imperial expansion. (10)

- World political and military domination was increased, despite constant conflicts.

- Britain enjoyed huge commercial gains. Colonies supplied cheap raw materials to be manufactured both for domestic and overseas markets.

- Colonial possessions enabled Britain to develop global trade patterns, thus increasing commercial revenue.

- Capitalism spread, to Britain's benefit. Britain exported technology, Parliamentary institutions, Christianity, her very language and even cricket, all of which increased her world influence.

- Britain felt that she was doing good by sending her skills, such as in education and medicine, to under-developed areas.

- The Empire enriched British society through contact with a variety of world cultures and some absorption of their particular elements.

3. (a) Describe the most important achievements of Florence Nightingale. (20)

- Bored by the lack of opportunities for women of her comfortable social status, Florence visited hospitals at home and abroad.

- The idea of nursing training grew after 1815, particularly in the German Empire. A centre opened at Kaiserwerth (1836). Florence trained there as a sick nurse.

- Sent to the British hospital at Scutari after the outbreak of the Crimean War (1854), Florence was appalled at the dirty conditions.

- A great administrator, she worked hard to improve them. Supported by Palmerston, she cut through red tape and reformed medical services.

- She insisted on absolute cleanliness, applying principles of fresh air, soap and water, and stressing the importance of providing the correct conditions for patient recovery. She promoted the idea that nursing was far more than doling out medicines.

- In just a few weeks at Scutari, during 1855, she reduced the death-rate from 42% to 24%. A legend grew up around her as 'The Lady with the Lamp'. She used this to further her work after the war.

- After 1856, she reformed the army medical services, leading to the establishment, at Netley Hospital, of the Army Nursing Service (1881).

- Florence developed nursing education. In 1860, the Nightingale School of Nursing was set up at St Thomas's Hospital, London.

- She raised the status of nursing, leading to its being recognised as a vocation with proper professional standards.

- Abroad, she did much to improve sanitary conditions in India.

(b) Explain what impact she had on British society. (10)

- Professional nursing was of great public benefit.

- From the first training centre in London, nurses moved out to other hospitals, spreading improved nursing care throughout the country.

- Her long-term impact was widespread on British society. Long before the germ theory of disease advanced by Pasteur and others, Florence's observations in the Crimea had convinced her that dirt caused disease. This added greatly to the effectiveness of contemporary medical discoveries.

- The design and improvement of hospitals benefited from Florence's suggestions, making an increasingly positive public impact as infirmaries sprang up in developing urban centres.

- Not only her practical work, but her many publications, helped the cause of British medicine to the ultimate benefit of the nation.

4. (a) Describe the main features of the career of Charles Darwin. (20)

- Having given up medical studies at Edinburgh, Darwin went to Cambridge where his interest in nature study was turned into serious science.

- Darwin made a voyage on *The Beagle* (1831–1836), studying geology, botany and zoology. Through his detailed observation of plants on the islands of the Pacific Ocean, he noticed differences between species on different islands.

- He began to form his theories of evolution, or natural selection. First, that small variations in a species may be passed on by hereditary change, gradually causing change within that species.

- Secondly, taking the idea that all forms of life have to struggle to exist, he came to believe that those which best adapted themselves to their environment survived.

- Darwin modified his thinking during the 1840s. In 1859 came his *Origin of Species*, containing his evolutionary theories. This became one of the world's most famous books.

- In 1871, his *Descent of Man* showed that men and apes had a common ancestry.

- His theories met violent opposition, especially from the Church, fearing an undermining of the Biblical account of Creation and perhaps even of all religious belief.

- In a famous debate, Darwin's ideas were attacked by Samuel Wilberforce, bishop of Oxford. Nevertheless, Darwinism triumphed.

- Living quietly in Kent, Darwin wrote on a variety of scientific subjects, from the formation of vegetable mould by worms, to the standard textbook on barnacles.

- He died in 1882, universally recognised as an important scientist.

(b) Explain the importance of Darwin both in his own time and in today's world.　　(10)

- In his own day, Darwin's work transformed biological science. The arguments he stimulated raised the profile of scientific debate.

- Darwinism represented an important challenge to contemporary thinking, especially that of the Church with its belief in a single act of creation with all things shaped in their final, unchangeable form.

- His work laid foundations for others. Darwin did not explain how hereditary change worked. This was suggested by Mendel in his laws of heredity (1866).

- Research continued leading to the discovery, at Cambridge in 1953 by Crick and Watson, of a genetic code – the exact mechanism through which inheritance occurs.

- Detailed genetic work advances today through studies of the human genome.

5. (a) Describe the most important points in the career of Charles Dickens.　　(20)

- Born in Portsmouth in 1812, son of a navy Pay Office clerk, Charles Dickens had an insecure childhood. At one point, his father was thrown into the Marshalsea Prison for debt.

- Dickens moved to Chatham and then London in 1822. This featured as the setting for many of his books.

- After working in a blacking warehouse, he was sent off to school before being articled to a solicitor in 1827.

- He learnt shorthand working as a reporter in the law courts and in Parliament. He wrote magazine articles and then turned to novels. Many of his early experiences provided him with realistic material for his writing.

- His most famous novels include *Oliver Twist* (1837–1839), *The Old Curiosity Shop* (1840–1841), *A Christmas Carol* (1843), *David Copperfield* (1849–1850) and *Great Expectations* (1860–1861).

- Dickens also wrote historical stories such as *Barnaby Rudge* (1841), set during the Gordon Riots (1780) and *A Tale of Two Cities* (1859) with a background of the French Revolution.

- After visiting the USA, Dickens published his *American Notes* (1842), detailing his travel experiences.

- His reflections on American life also featured in *Martin Chuzzlewit* (1843–1844).

101

- At his death, in 1870, Dickens was famous for his literary masterpieces. He was a popular, widely-read author and noted as a perceptive social critic, seeing life from the point of view of the urban poor.

(b) Explain how he made an impact on his own times. (10)

- In his novels, Dickens protested against the cruelty and selfishness of industrial England. His portrayal of social abuses helped the cause of reform.

- Using his popularity, he campaigned against many contemporary institutions such as the 1834 Poor Law system, the law itself, harsh prison conditions and the civil service. His views thus gained widespread appeal.

- Dickens achieved a broad readership because he was a great storyteller and entertainer. He created many memorable characters like Mr Pickwick and Ebenezer Scrooge, who caught the popular imagination.

- He achieved success through his skilful monthly publication of some of his works in serial form.

- Dickens travelled about giving highly popular public readings of his books.

- His influence also spread through others. Thomas Carlyle developed Dickens's idea that revolution and disorder may follow on from political and social injustices.

6. (a) Describe the main details of the Unification of Germany 1862–1871. (20)

- After 1862, Bismarck, Minister-President of Prussia, wanted to unite Germany under Prussian control. Following a policy of 'blood and iron', Bismarck first isolated his enemies diplomatically, then crushed them in war.

- In 1863, the duchy of Schleswig was declared part of Denmark under a new constitution. Bismarck interfered to gain the support of Germans within Schleswig.

- He began his diplomacy. Russia was friendly with Prussia owing to Prussian support against a Polish rebellion in 1863.

- Promises of territory along the Rhine assured French neutrality. Britain, anxious about Russia and France, did nothing to aid the Danes. Austria was asked to help Prussia.

- Austria and Prussia invaded Denmark, overcoming the Danes. By the Convention of Gastein (1865), Prussia gained Schleswig. Austria acquired Holstein.

- Bismarck now aimed to defeat Austria. He secured French neutrality and Italian support, promising them territories in the Rhineland and Venetia.

- Austria was provoked into war. Defeated at Sadowa after only seven weeks of fighting, Austria received easy terms at the Treaty of Prague (1866). Bismarck wanted Austrian help against France.

- Prussia formed a North German Confederation of states north of the Main, and then moved on France. Austria and Italy were friendly with Prussia. Russian support was gained through backing her Black Sea claims. Bismarck persuaded the South German states that France had her eye on their territories.

- In 1870, Bismarck goaded France into war through his alterations to the Ems Telegram, concerning the succession of a German prince to the Spanish throne.

- After defeats at Metz, Sedan and the Siege of Paris, the French surrendered. Under the Treaty of Frankfurt (1871), France paid reparations to Germany and lost Alsace and Lorraine.

- In January 1871, at Versailles, the German Empire was proclaimed.

(b) Explain how German unification affected Britain. (10)

- Britain became concerned. Bismarck had established Germany as the most powerful state in Europe.

- Germany's rapid industrial growth threatened Britain's economic supremacy. Competition increased as Germany built up her colonial possessions.

- The growth of German imperialism, nationalism and militarism generated tensions which helped cause war in 1914.

- Britain was worried by a state where force, rather than ideas, seemed to shape the basis of government. Germany had a strong, military monarchy. Its power rested on the sword. Britain had to be watchful.

7. (a) Describe the causes, details and effects of the Irish potato famine between 1845 and 1851. (20)

- The famine was caused by the recurrent failure of the potato crop owing to blight, a disease reducing potatoes to black slime.

- The Irish relied too much on one crop – the potato – so when that failed, disaster struck.

- Blight destroyed about 50% of the crop in 1845 and 75% in 1846.

- Crop yields recovered in 1847, but any benefits were wiped out as less land was cultivated. Thus, the harvest remained poor.

- The potato crop failed completely in 1848.

- People starved. Famished peasants died by the roadside or in their cottages.

- 1846–1850 saw the death-rate increase. About 1 million people died of starvation or disease. During famine years, birth-rates fell.

- Death and emigration depopulated Ireland. About 250,000 people moved to England. One million went to America. The population dropped from 8 million in 1815 to 4 million by 1851.

- Many small peasant farmers were ruined. Unable to pay their rents they were evicted. Farmers with larger landholdings dominated the countryside.

- The English government repealed the Corn Laws so that grain could reach Ireland. However, the starving Irish could not afford to buy it.

- Government help was limited to those with farms no larger than one quarter of an acre, meaning that many starved.

- Public-work schemes were established, paying men for labour in order to buy food. Charities set up soup kitchens.

(b) Explain the impact of this famine on Anglo-Irish relations in the second half of
the 19th century. (10)

- Anglo-Irish relations worsened. The English showed a lack of sympathy, believing that the famine conditions were exaggerated. Irish attitudes towards England hardened.

- England offered too little too late. This angered the Irish, many of whom believed that more could have been done sooner. The inaction of the British government soured relations.

- The famine heightened the Irish land problem, which became a major issue after about 1850.

- Demands for home rule were fired up by memories of the famine. Irish reformers saw political independence as their only way to social and economic reform.

- English politicians like Gladstone were forced to suggest schemes for improvement such as the Land Acts (1870, 1881) and the Home Rule Bill (1886), but not until Wyndham's Land Purchase Act (1903) was there any real benefit for the Irish.

Appendix – ISEB Common Entrance 13+ Mark Scheme

Evidence Questions

Question 1: Comprehension of source (2 marks)
This will be a simple comprehension question based on Source A.

Question 2: Comprehension of source (3 marks)
This will look at Source B and ask a more demanding comprehension question.

Question 3: Corroboration by cross-referencing sources (7 marks)
This will call for a comparison of all three sources.

Question 4: Evaluation of sources for utility/consideration of provenance (8 marks)
This question will investigate the usefulness of sources. It will also ask about provenance in some form: how/who wrote the sources, or when the sources were written, or whether the nationality of the writer might make a difference as to the reliability of the sources.

Essay Questions

SELECTIVE DESCRIPTION e.g. *Describe the key features of … etc.*		
Mark	**Target**	**Causation/recall of knowledge**
1–8	Level 1	Simple statements offering some features/ideas supported by some knowledge, embryonic, inaccurate or irrelevant knowledge; lacking real coherence and structure.
9–15	Level 2	More developed statements giving features supported by more relevant knowledge; thinly substantiated passages; uncertain overall structure.
16–20	Level 3	Developed selection of features with sound substantiation and structure; good range of features; for top of level, answer will show clear linkage and relevant importance of features.

EVALUATION / ANALYSIS e.g. *Explain why…*		
Mark	**Target**	**Evaluation of factors against one another/definitions of success and failure/contextual assessment**
1–4	Level 1	Simple statement offering basic and largely unfocused opinion.
5–8	Level 2	More developed analysis with some coherent judgement; some substantiation of assertions.
9–10	Level 3	Precisely selected knowledge in a clear framework of argument; strong and developed analysis/assessment with cogent judgements; strong substantiation of assertions.

   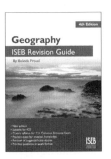
 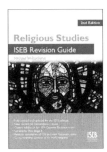  

    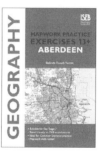

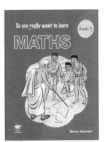